THE BO
AND AUG

'...another fine addition to the 'Great Battles' series published by Windrush Press'
The Irish Times

'This attractively produced book...will appeal primarily to those with an interest in military history who should be delighted with the sketch-maps and the extensive lists of regiments in appendices. For the general reader...there are plenty of interesting details.'
The Church of Ireland Gazette

THE AUTHOR

John Kinross is a former publisher's publicity man who worked at *Country Life* magazine. He is the author of *Discovering Battlefields of England* and the more recent *Walking and Exploring the Battlefields of Britain*. On retirement he took a Naval History MA at Exeter University. He is a keen member of the Battlefield Trust and the Fortress Society of Great Britain. John is married and lives a cannon shot away from the battlefield of Sedgemoor.

Other titles in the GREAT BATTLES series
Hastings by Peter Poyntz Wright
Agincourt by Christopher Hibbert
Edgehill 1642 by Peter Young
Marston Moor 1644 by Peter Young
Trafalgar: The Nelson Touch by David Howarth
Corunna by Christopher Hibbert
Wellington's Peninsular Victories by Michael Glover
Waterloo: A Near Run Thing by David Howarth
Arnhem by Christopher Hibbert

Other Military Books published by The Windrush Press
The Recollections of Rifleman Harris
Edited and Introduced by Christopher Hibbert
The Letters of Private Wheeler
Edited and with a Foreword by B.H. Liddell Hart
The Diaries of a Napoleonic Foot Soldier
Edited and Introduced by Mark Raeff
A Soldier of the 71st
Edited and Introduced by Christopher Hibbert
The Wheatley Diary
Edited and Introduced by Christopher Hibbert
The Recollections of Sergeant Morris
Edited by John Selby

THE BOYNE AND AUGHRIM

THE WAR OF THE TWO KINGS

JOHN KINROSS

THE WINDRUSH PRESS · GLOUCESTERSHIRE

First published in Great Britain by
The Windrush Press in 1997
Reprinted 1998
Little Window, High Street,
Moreton-in-Marsh
Gloucestershire GL56 0LL
Tel: 01608 652012
Fax: 01608 652125

British Library in Cataloguing Data
A catalogue record for this book is available from the British Library

ISBN 1 900624 07 9

Typeset by Archetype, Condicote, Cheltenham
http://www.archetype-it.com
Printed and bound by Interprint Limited, Malta

The front cover shows a detail from *The Battle of the Boyne, 1690* by Benjamin West
by courtesy of Peter Newark's Military Pictures
Cover design by Miranda Harvey

To the Memory of A.J.H.

Contents

List of Illustrations and Maps

List of Maps and Plans

All maps and plans drawn by R.W. Naesmyth

List of Illustrations

Foreword

This book would still be on the drawing board if it had not been for two people. Firstly, Victoria Huxley who commissioned it and has patiently waited for it to materialise. Secondly, my friend Joe Gallagher of the Irish Tourist Board, who guided me round both the Boyne and Aughrim.

I am indebted to Major R.W. Naesmyth of Posso RA, rtd., who drew the maps and family tree, to Baron Robbert Van Heeckeren who made several suggestions, to the Smit family of Mook who took me to Het Loo, to Brigadier K. Timbers of the Royal Artillery Institute and Dr H. Murtagh who advised on Aughrim. I would also like to thank the staff of the Battle Centre at Aughrim for their kindness, the staff of the Kildare Street library in Dublin and the anonymous lady who opened the window on a hot day, the staff of the RMC library at Sandhurst and the new Central Library in Taunton, where much of the book was written.

Finally, I must thank my wife for doing without our dining room table for about six months and my son for his help with computer research and all the members of the BATS Bureau who prepared the disk for printing.

John Kinross
Burrowbridge
October, 1996

Author's Note

The dates in this book follow the old style calendar contemporary with the events described.

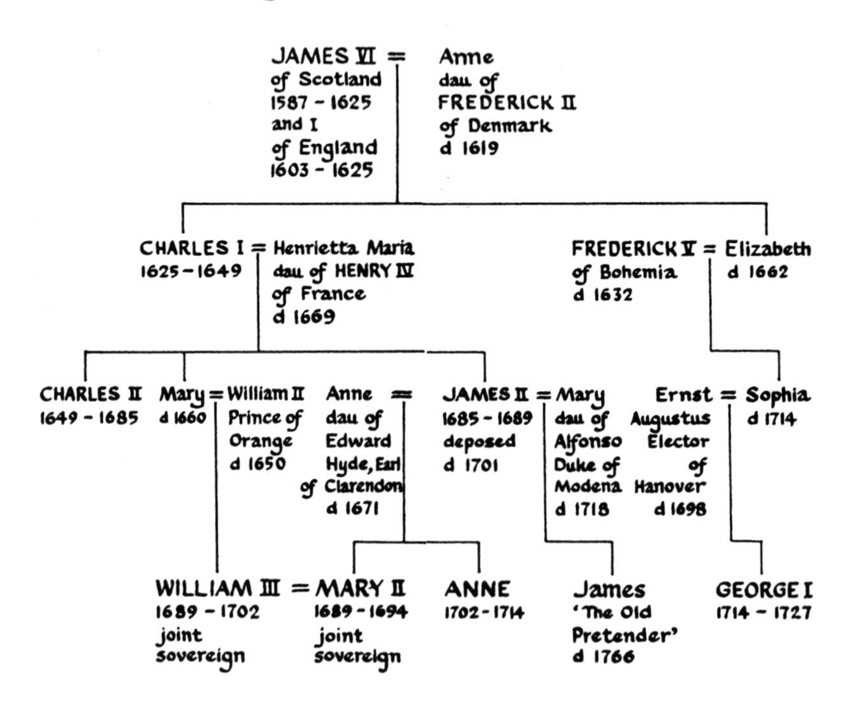
HOUSE OF STUART
Showing Orange and Hanoverian Connections
JAMES VI = Anne
of Scotland 1587 - 1625 and I of England 1603 - 1625
dau of FREDERICK II of Denmark d 1619
CHARLES I = Henrietta Maria
1625-1649
dau of HENRY IV of France d 1669
FREDERICK V = Elizabeth
of Bohemia d 1632
d 1662
CHARLES II
1649 - 1685
Mary = William II
d 1660
Prince of Orange d 1650
Anne = JAMES II
dau of Edward Hyde, Earl of Clarendon d 1671
JAMES II = Mary
1685 - 1689 deposed d 1701
dau of Alfonso Duke of Modena d 1718
Ernst Augustus = Sophia
Elector of Hanover d 1698
d 1714
WILLIAM III = MARY II
1689 - 1702 joint sovereign
1689 - 1694 joint sovereign
ANNE
1702 - 1714
James
'The Old Pretender' d 1766
GEORGE I
1714 - 1727

1

Prelude to the Irish Campaign

No prelude to the Battles of the Boyne and Aughrim can commence without looking closely at the two main characters concerned. King James II succeeded his brother, Charles II, in 1685. He was then aged fifty-two, the same age as his contemporary, Samuel Pepys. His portrait shows a man of moderate stature, shorter than his brother Charles, with eyes downcast and wide apart, the same proud nose as Charles but a rather downcast and cruel mouth. As a youngster he had followed his father round the Civil War battles and at an early age had been trained as a soldier. He fought for the French in Marshal Turenne's army and only in 1656 was he forced to resign, when Commonwealth England made a treaty with France and part of the wording insisted that the royal prince should not serve in the French army. So James followed his brother to the Spanish Netherlands, where for a time he fought with their army against Turenne. He distinguished himself at the Battle of the Dunes, but his courage did not seem to last beyond his youth. At the Restoration in 1660 he was made Lord High Admiral, and at once he set to with Pepys to restore the English fleet. The latter though was sharp to recognise that the Duke of York, as he then was, was easily led by others, and had a fondness for the Irish, which is apparent in the entry in Pepys' Diary for December, 1664:

> It seems of all mankind, there is no man so led by another as the Duke of York is by my Lord Muskerry, [son of the Earl of Clancarty and killed the following year in a battle with the Dutch] and this Fitzharding. In as much as, when the King, Charles II, would have him be Privy Purse, the Duke wept and said, 'But sir, I must have your promise if you will have my dear Charles [Lord Muskerry] from me, that if ever you have occasion for an army again, I may have him with me; believing him to be the best commander of an army in the world.' But Mr Chomley [friend of Pepys] thinks, as all other men I meet do, that he [Muskerry] is a very ordinary fellow. It is strange how the Duke do love naturally, and affect the Irish above the English.

The duke though lost his popularity rapidly when he openly became

William III by an unknown artist

Mary II by William Wissing

a Roman Catholic. This was similar to becoming a Fascist in England in the 1930s. He also had an expensive wife, Anne Hyde, and a number of mistresses. By 1667 his brother was forced to appoint three commissioners to keep an eye on the duke's estate. These were Lord Berkeley of Stratton (on the Devon/Cornwall border), Colonel Werden and Colonel Anthony Eyre. The duke must have known two of these men well as they had served in the army with him, so it is unlikely that the extravagance of his household at Audley End was curtailed. It was one thing as heir to the throne being a Catholic, a spendthrift, a man who clung to unsuitable advisers and who wept in public. It was entirely different when that duke became King of England.

William of Orange was a very different character. Born in 1650 he had the advantage of youth. He was a Dutch Protestant – his chapel at Het Loo Palace in Holland is plain and simple, just a few benches and a reader's desk – and he was a man of few words. His early upbringing was mostly in the saddle and his father, William II, had a struggle to keep the United Provinces from dominance by France and from falling out with each other. His mother, Mary Stuart, was a sister of Charles II and of James II, so he was cousin to James, but the two did not see eye-to-eye from an early age. William is usually shown on horseback in paintings or sculptures. However the Kneller portrait in Williamsburg shows a short man in a long wig, with a long face, sharp eyes and a strong chin. He is standing hand-in-hand with his wife, Mary, daughter of Anne and James II, shortly after their marriage in 1677. Mary is one of the most pleasing of all Stuarts. Intensely loyal to her husband, she was happiest dashing about Hampton Court arranging flowers and seeing to the decoration, ignoring her anxious maids and lady dressers attempts to persuade her back into her room to complete her dressing. She proved to be a very capable leader of the country in William's absence and her early death was a tragedy both for William and the country.

William had friends in both Whig and Tory parties in England. Danby, a Tory, had been the instigator of his marriage as he was keen to see the English army supporting Holland against France. The Whigs under Shaftesbury were keen to support the illegitimate Duke of Monmouth, son of Charles II and Lucy Walter, in his claim to the throne. However Monmouth was, with Shaftesbury, involved in the Rye House Plot of 1683, in which a group of Whigs decided to kill Charles II and his brother at a house of that name, and both were banished abroad.

At the age of twenty-two William found himself Commander-in-Chief of the Dutch forces and he soon learnt that only an alliance with other states against the might of Louis XIV's France would save Holland from being overwhelmed. The Whigs wanted William to support the

Exclusion Bill, banning James from the succession, but William was content to wait. He first of all had to decide what support he should give to the Duke of Monmouth, who on James's becoming king in 1685, had planned an invasion of the West Country. He watched the luckless Monmouth set sail for England in July 1685 with three small ships and a handful of men, some of whom were to figure in the Irish war to come. The Monmouth campaign that ended tragically on the field of Sedgemoor near Bridgwater after only twenty-one days was a warning to William. James's small army was efficient and well led. One particular officer, though only second-in-command, was to feature prominently in the history of the British Army in the years to come.

This was John Churchill, future Duke of Marlborough. Also born in 1650, Churchill was a fine horseman, successful soldier and his wife, Sarah, was a close friend of Princess Anne, James II's second daughter. Firmly in the Protestant camp, Anne had married Prince George of Denmark, so William had an ally in England. He had strong contacts with that country and in the Irish war a mercenary army under the Duke of Wurtemberg of four thousand, five hundred Danish troops fought for him with distinction.

William was in a tricky position with regard to his father-in-law. When James asked for the six English and Scottish regiments in Holland under Dutch pay to be returned; he obeyed with alacrity and even offered to lead them in person.

William relied on spies to ferret out information for him on Jacobite intrigues. One of his letters, written in bad English, can be seen in Hampton Court Palace to one Henry Ferne, sending him £5,100 for his services. The date is 17 June 1701 but Ferne had been working for him since 1684. This was a considerable amount of money. The sum of £1000 then was about £60,000 in today's currency so even if Ferne was only given one payment, he could well retire on over £300,000.

William had watched the Monmouth ships sail and land their small army with ease in the West Country. The famous Protestant Wind that took his large fleet the same way in 1688 was also lucky, both in helping him avoid the English fleet, and in landing at Torbay without interruption.

The English Revolution that led to James's hurried departure from England to France has been described in many books and it is not intended to go into details here. Surprisingly though it was the sudden and unexpected arrival of a new prince that caused chaos in the Protestant ranks of both politicians and soldiers. When Anne Hyde died in 1673, James had married Mary of Modena, a Catholic princess who was close to the court of King Louis XIV. She had no children until suddenly in

1688 a son was born. The disillusioned Tories joined with the Whig leaders and invited William and Mary to invade England to save their country's law and religion.

James's soldiers deserted to William's camp as the Williamite army under the portly Marshal Schomberg slowly made its way from Torbay towards London. Only James's Irish troops proved loyal to him. There was a brief skirmish at Wincanton, where a troop of Jacobite horse under Patrick Sarsfield, more of whom we shall hear later, got the better of a Williamite troop of cavalry.

This did not stop the defection to William's camp of John Churchill and later Prince George of Denmark. The usually brave James suffered from a nosebleed. His army at Salisbury disintegrated just when a shadow of firmness might have carried the day.

The English Parliament passed a resolution in 1688, after James had fled to France with his queen and son, stating:

> King James II having endeavoured to subvert the constitution of the kingdom by breaking the original contract between King and people, and, by the advice of Jesuits and other wicked persons, having violated the fundamental laws, and having withdrawn himself out of the kingdom, had abdicated the government and that the throne had thereby become vacant.

On 13 February 1689 the Lords and Commons, headed by George Savile, Marquess of Halifax, offered the crown of England jointly to William and Mary. It was duly accepted and James became an outlaw. To his many Jacobite supporters however he was still their king.

There are some stains on William's character and his reign. In 1692 the Scottish chiefs had been required to swear allegiance to their new sovereign in front of a sheriff before the first day of January. The small Macdonald clan in Glencoe were far from a sheriff and it was mid-winter. The Campbells of Glenlyon were the nearest troops to Glencoe. They were given written orders to demand that those who didn't obey be put to the sword. These were signed it is thought by William, though others say it was the Master of Stair, John Dalrymple, who signed them on the king's behalf. The order went to Colonel Campbell of Glenlyon, who was only too keen to obey it as the Campbells and Macdonalds were traditional enemies. The resulting massacre of thirty-one Macdonalds including their leader was never forgotten. Hamilton who had passed the order from Stair to Campbell, fled the country. Parliament debated the matter in detail and the Master of Stair was dismissed from his secretaryship. Glenlyon went to Bruges, where he died in 1696. William did not allow the event to upset him, but he never went to Scotland. On the day of his death, 8 March 1702, the bells of St Giles played the tune 'Wilful Willie' and a Highland widow announced to her neighbour that she knew what had happened as that day her cow gave twice as much milk as she had had from her in the last seven years.

The final picture though must rest with the Convention Parliament that, with the House of Lords, put Mary and William on the throne. They were men of great ability. The House of Commons chose Richard Hampden, son of the famous Buckinghamshire Parliamentarian who had lost his life after his wound at Chalgrove Field, as its chairman. He was ably supported by men like Gilbert Dolben, son of the late Archbishop of York, Wharton, Sawyer and Christopher Musgrave. The country MPs included no less a person than the great mathematician, Isaac Newton. The Speaker, Powle and Halifax from the Lords finally came up with the decision that William and Mary should become king and queen of England for their joint and separate lives, and that, during their joint lives, the administration of the government should be by the prince alone. The succession was to be settled on the posterity of Mary, then of Anne and her children and then on William, and his children. Presumably this meant that if Mary died first, as she did, and William married again then any children by a second marriage would have prior claim to the throne before Anne. This did not happen and it was tragic for Anne that none of her many children survived her. No mention was made of James's son, born without witnesses just before his abdication. Thus the Jacobite pretenders were able to remain a threat to the British throne for the next fifty years, especially in Scotland.

The British government was under no less than four different alliance agreements at the start of the war in Ireland and four more in 1690. These were:

1. Agreement to join the Dutch and English fleets of April 1689.
2. Agreement with the States General to an offensive and defensive league by sea and land as from August 1689.
3. Agreement between the Emperor [Leopold of Habsburg] and States General of May 1689, which England joined making a triple alliance from September 1689.
4. Alliance between the Emperor, King William and the King of Spain [King Charles] of December 1689.
5. Agreement between England and Frederick, Elector of Brandenburg of May 1690 with a secret clause to assist each other with a sufficient number of men in case of invasion.

6. An agreement between England and Denmark dated November 1690, with an article to assist each other with a number of men in case of invasion. This agreement had nothing to do with the Danish troops that fought for William in Ireland who were virtually hired as mercenaries.
7. An agreement dated October 1690, between England, Savoy and the States General with a secret clause for the restoration of the Vaudois [an area centred on Lausanne, Switzerland, formerly part of Savoy].
8. An agreement between England, States General and the Duke of Hanover of June 1692 to supply Hanover with 7,940 men – horse, foot and dragoons. This was the first of the Hanover agreements which naturally became more common in the reigns of the three Georges.

Thus William was anxious not to have to renege on these agreements and it is surprising that it took his government until November 1692 before Sir Thomas Clarges got up in Parliament and said that England had to pay 20,000 crowns a month to Savoy and the Dutch only half that amount, whereas in the past contributions had been equal. Nothing seems to have come of this complaint. William was still a Dutchman and it is likely that even at this stage in his career, the first priority was the safety of the country of his birth. Nevertheless by 1689 William had successfully acquired the English throne, but in Ireland there was trouble.

2

Ireland in the 1690s and Tyrconnell

The persecution of the Catholics in Ireland was followed by a relatively calm period during the reign of Charles II. Many Irish landowners, both Catholic and Protestant had followed Charles into exile on the continent. Amongst them was James Butler, Duke of Ormond. A capable man, he had commanded the loyal forces against the rebels in the 1641 rising. He was made Lord Lieutenant by King Charles I, but was defeated by Cromwell and escaped to join young Charles on the continent. He returned as Lord Lieutenant at the Restoration and ensured the Acts of Settlement in 1662 by which those Irish landowners who had been abroad during the Commonwealth received back their land. However, Ormond soon discovered that those Cromwellians who had stayed on in Ireland were naturally reluctant to give up land to incoming Catholics.

The Irish people were, according to the Bishop of Derry, mostly Catholic or, in the north, Presbyterian. Neither of these groups supported the small Church of Ireland. There were also Quakers, like Sir William Penn, father of William Penn, who had an estate in Cork. The Catholics and dissenters were not permitted to take part in politics, the army or in public service. Yet they constituted at least 75 per cent of the population of about 2.2 million in 1687. Tyrconnell was to change this of course, but the 'Old English' families, mostly Catholic, like the Talbots, Luttrells and Plunketts owned at least two-thirds of the land. Ormond belonged to this group – he was a Butler – but supported the established Church of Ireland. The 'New English' group, mostly Scots from the west coast of Scotland or English dissenters, settled in Ulster and some had considerable military experience or aptitude, as was soon to be discovered.

Jonathan Swift summed up the strange situation as: 'The Catholics of Ireland lost their estates for fighting in defence of their king, while those who cut off his head and forced the son to fly for his life got the very estates the Catholics lost.'

It was indeed bizarre. Meanwhile the Gaels or native Catholics tried to get back the land which centuries ago had been taken by the Old English, regardless of the religion of these landed gentry. The word logic does not come into the land settlement. In fact to talk about Irish politics and logic together is probably an indication that the speaker has

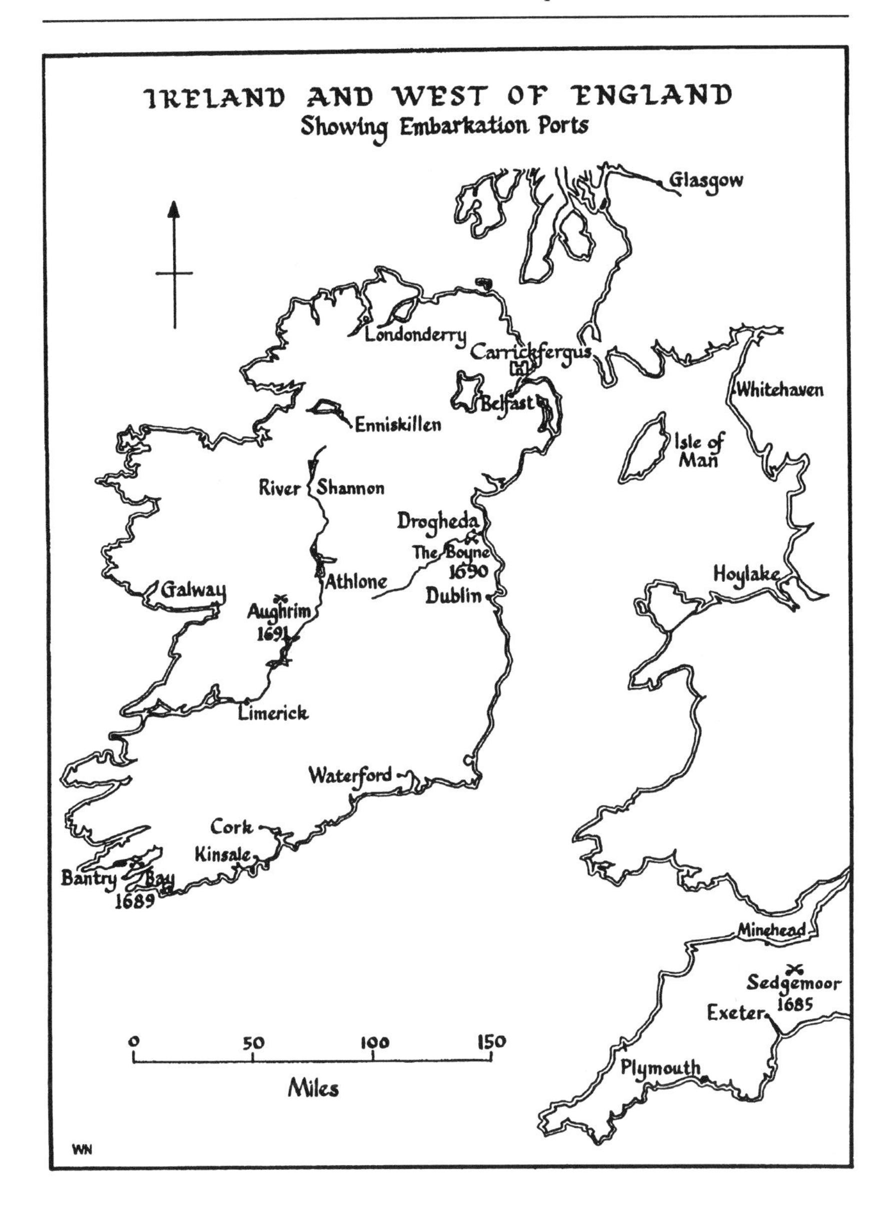

never been there. Charles II had done his best with the problem. An Act of Explanation and an Act of Settlement by the Irish Parliament in his reign had permitted some Catholics to get back their estates, but by the end of his reign the Catholics still only owned 22 per cent of the land and that mostly in the far west.

Ormond compromised and Catholic priests were allowed to practise their religion and, west of the Shannon, the Catholics were permitted to own land. As soon as James II came to the English throne however, Ormond was recalled and Henry Hyde, 2nd Earl of Clarendon* replaced him. However, Ormond had been both general and head of the administration, while Clarendon was only an administrator. A new figure now emerges as head of the Irish forces.

This was Richard Talbot, later the Earl of Tyrconnell, who was the youngest son of Sir William Talbot and Alison Netterville – as they had sixteen children the family tree is quite complex. Sir William was Recorder of Dublin and in 1613 a member of the Irish Parliament. Richard was born in 1630 and was brought up on the large family estate. He was eleven when the Irish insurrection under Owen O'Neill started and young Richard became a standard bearer in Dongan's Regiment against the Parliamentary troops. Later he was made a cornet in Preston's Horse and fought with the Confederates against the Parliamentarians at Dungan Hill (1647) where he was taken prisoner. The young Talbots were brought up as loyal Catholics, loyal to their king, provided he was Catholic and above all, loyal Irish. He was not above making his own fortune if he could, even at others' expense. In old age Richard became stout and suffered from frequent illness, but his mind remained clear until his death.

Tyrconnell's strengths were that he was capable of foreseeing the problems of the Irish army. He knew that there were shortages of arms, money, ammunition and other supplies. He was prepared to go to great lengths to obtain these things and crossed over to France to get them. He had to keep hotheads like Sarsfield, more of an enemy than a friend, under control and during his absence in France before Aughrim, he was away from September 1690 to January 1691, he was missed by his colleagues. Although Sarsfield considered himself in command, there were others who missed Tyrconnell and welcomed him back. His weaknesses were that he made enemies, he was ruthless and not afraid to promote his own career before anything else, but he did put Ireland and the old Catholic families first and, had he lived, he would not have been keen on the lack of tolerance shown by those in command after the Treaty of Limerick.

James created him Earl in 1685 and later Duke of Tyrconnell. Tyrconnell sent 3,000 Irish troops to England in 1688, but they mostly returned and could not prevent William's landing in 1688. When James had recovered from his disaster in England he built up an army in France to support Tyrconnell. Some money had already been sent to arm Tyrconnell's

* Henry Hyde, 2nd Earl of Clarendon, was the brother of Anne Hyde, James's first wife.

Richard Talbot, Earl of Tyrconnell, on an English playing card shown as the knave giving weapons to Irish Catholics

Tyrconnell's name remembered today as a brand of Irish whiskey

recruits but it was not until March 1689 that James's army was ready. It was in King Louis's interests to carry out a war in Ireland, for if he could tie down William and his army there, preferably for a long time, the supply of troops to the anti-French army in the Netherlands would dry up and the French forces would be free to roam where they wanted.

Under Tyrconnell's influence Catholic judges replaced Protestants. In the army, Tyrconnell investigated anyone who had fought for Cromwell and Catholic officers soon replaced Protestants. The local government officials were Protestants especially in Dublin and Belfast, and there was no easy way Tyrconnell could replace them as this was Clarendon's business. The problem, and one of the main causes of the war in Ireland, was land.

Clarendon worked out a scheme whereby landowners in possession were to compensate Catholics who were without their former property. This was a sane plan perhaps, but one that considerably upset the Protestant Irish, who had had the best of the previous twenty-five years. Cromwellian settlers under the Act of Explanation (1665) had to surrender a third of their holdings to form a pool for compensating Catholics. This pleased neither side as Protestant landowners objected to having to give away hard-earned land and Catholics obviously wanted more, and they resented the 'Old English' landowners getting priority over native Irish. This system depended of course on how it was administered and it never really had a chance of success, as in March 1689 James II crossed over to Ireland with, eventually, a total of 7,000 French troops, money and arms. Tyrconnell had been depicted in the same set of playing cards that had shown the Monmouth rising, as arming the Irish Catholics and he found nearly 30,000 of them prepared to fight. They were poorly shod and apart from French arms, had little apart from their loyalty to the Catholic cause to fight for. The Protestants either fled the country or joined up with the defenders of Enniskillen and Londonderry.

Thus war was a certainty. The overwhelming army of Louis XIV of France was responsible for moving the chess pieces about Europe. No king of France has ever claimed such fame as Louis. King from the age of four, he left the control of his country to Cardinal Mazarin. When the cardinal died in 1661, Louis, then just twenty-three, took complete command. He ruled with a very small council of state, leaving the war policy to the Marquis de Louvois, the finances to Colbert, and the control of foreign affairs to the Marquis de Pomponne. He took a great delight in giving orders and in the general glory of being king. He was frequently quarrelling with the pope, especially Pope Innocent XI, over the royal right of appointments to benefices.

Louis's foreign policy kept him at loggerheads with William of Orange.

He took advantage of the death of his father-in-law, King Philip IV of Spain, to attack the Spanish Netherlands, and, at the Treaty of Aix-la-Chapelle, he gained some valuable towns in the Spanish Netherlands, namely Charleroi, Binch, Ath, Douai, Tournai, Oudenarde, Lille, Armentières, Courtrai, Bergues and Furnes. He surrendered Franche-Comté, St Omer and Aire but under a secret treaty with Emperor Leopold he agreed to have them back on the death of Charles II.

Charles had formed a Triple Alliance with Sweden and the United Provinces to keep Louis at bay. However Louis set about undermining this agreement. By a secret treaty at Dover in 1670 he persuaded Charles II to fight the Dutch in exchange for a considerable sum of money. He bought off Sweden and entered into a long-lasting agreement with the Elector of Bavaria.

Thus England went to war with the Dutch and suffered the ignomy of losing two naval battles against De Ruyter's fleet until the English Parliament successfully persuaded Charles to make peace with them in 1674, though the war between France and the United Provinces continued until the Peace of Nijmegen in 1678–1679. Thus Louis obtained Franche-Comté, Alsace, Lorraine, Freiburg and Breisach. The real gains were made by England though, for peace with the Dutch meant the majority of the sea transport trade of the Dutch marine now passed to England. England also gained New Amsterdam, which soon became New York and the Island of St Helena, which was eventually to become a prison for Napoleon.

The Turks were fighting against the Empire at the same time as Louis was expanding his eastern frontiers. They finally came to grief on the gates of Vienna in 1683, defeated by a combined army, led by King John Sobieski of Poland (an ancestor of Bonny Prince Charlie) and Charles V of Lorraine. Louis was by 1685 in a difficult situation. James II had just come to the throne of England. Should Louis, a fellow Catholic support him, thereby upsetting Protestants or should he not interfere and sit by and watch? He did neither of these things, but in 1685 by revoking the Edict of Nantes which had allowed freedom of worship in France, he upset the French Huguenots by no longer allowing them to practise their Protestant religion. These were merchants and traders, artisans and craftsmen whom France could ill afford to lose; they emigrated in thousands to England, Prussia and Holland taking their trades with them. Overnight many French industries were ruined and England gained in the same way she had gained in Elizabethan times after the St Bartholomew massacre. Not only were these incomers valuable workers, but they spread the hatred of popery in England, so that they helped pave the way towards the success of the 1688 revolution.

James II with Anne Hyde, his first Duchess
Sir Peter Lely

Louis XIV of France

The war that broke out in Ireland in 1689 was really an extension of the war of the Grand Alliance between William and Louis. William was not prepared to see England become the only Protestant part of the British Isles. He had to settle troubles in both Scotland and Ireland first. He left the army in Scotland under the command of General Mackay, an officer who played an important part in his Irish campaign, but who was well and truly defeated at Killiekrankie in July 1689. The Scottish Jacobites under Dundee were supported by a small Irish contingent under Colonel Cannon and included Camerons, Macdonalds, Macleans and Macdonells. They had a small number of horse, few firearms and very little supplies. Mackay had a train of packhorses, cavalry under Lords Belhaven and Annadale, some experienced border troops of Leven's regiment, Lord Hastings' Somerset regiment – their monument stands in Taunton today – and some inexperienced troops under Ramsay. The Highlanders caught them on the march from Pitlochry to Blair Atholl. Waiting until the sun was in his enemy's eyes, Dundee charged down on Mackay's troops. After a single fusillade, there was no time to fix bayonets before the Scottish claymores were on them. Mackay escaped with his horse and only the regiments of Hastings and Leven preserved any order. The rest were cut down and the stores captured. Dundee would have followed up this victory by hunting down the retreating Williamite army but he was dead. A sharpshooter, probably in Urrard House, had dispatched him at the hour of his victory like General Wolfe at Quebec.

Colonel Cannon who took over the Highlanders was no leader, and could not stop the Scots from quarrelling. The clans who had hesitated to join the battle now came in. The Robertsons were sent foraging but went too far and were cut down by dragoons at St Johnstone near Perth. The Highlanders moved on Dunkeld, held by Cleland and his Cameronian regiment. The Battle of Dunkeld lasted for four hours, unlike Killiekrankie that only took two minutes. The Cameronians beat off all attacks on their defended house, wall and church. They set fire to houses occupied by the Highlanders. Cleland and his second-in-command, Major Henderson, were both killed but Captain Monroe took command and the Highlanders were forced to withdraw. House to house fighting was not their strong point. The clans dispersed, the Irish went to Mull, the Lowlanders back to their homes and the Jacobites in Scotland had, for the time being at least, ceased to exist.

What is interesting in this campaign is that it showed that Jacobites needed good leaders. Fighting for their religion was not enough. Dundee was supreme but his deputy was useless. The Williamite troops at the Boyne lost their Marshal but it made no difference to them. James was always unlucky with his generals; had Dundee survived and then taken his army over to Ireland, the Boyne might have been a different battle. Mackay could not conquer the Scottish Jacobites, but he was allowed to escape and he had untried troops elsewhere in Scotland, like his dragoons in Perth. He was a professional soldier and one defeat was not going to finish his career. His Cameronian regiment lost two leaders but carried on under their third-in-command. No troops fought more bravely than those men at Dunkeld. The difference between the trained professional soldier and the amateur came to the fore. Like their Irish counterparts the Scots Highlanders were fine in victory, but not so good in defeat. They plundered what they could get and took it home for their families. Desertion was not considered a disgrace. Only when they were formed into professional regiments with pay, food and uniforms did they really show what good soldier material they were. The Wild Geese and the Highlanders fought together on battlefields all over the world in the following fifty or more years after Dunkeld and were admired by both friends and enemies.

The army of William of Orange contained mercenary soldiers like the Dutch contingent. Mackay's force had some Dutch troops and their Dutch colonel was killed in the retreat afterwards. The English officers resented the Dutch officers, similarly the Irish Jacobite officers did not get on with the French officers and vice-versa. Men like the Duke of Marlborough could cope with this problem, they used interpreters and staff officers. Men like Colonel Cannon could not. The war that was to erupt in Ireland was unusual in having so many different troops under so many different commanders. A German commanded the Danes, there were French troops on both sides, even Finnish troops fought for William. The struggle in Ireland was not a simple English Protestant versus Irish Catholic war, it was a European struggle between the forces of King Louis and the forces of King William. The native Irish often stood back and looked on or later conducted guerilla warfare on their own behalf. The Boyne and Aughrim together with the Cork and Kinsale campaigns were training grounds for men like Sarsfield and Marlborough. They were also training grounds for the Irish who fought for the French under Tallard, Villeroi, Vendôme and Villars.

The main instigator of war in Ireland in 1689 was Richard Talbot, Earl of Tyrconnell, whom James had made his Lord Deputy. An ardent Roman Catholic, Richard was thirty in 1660 when he sailed with Charles II and the Duke of York, in whose regiment he had become a lieutenant-colonel. On his arrival in London, he was made a Gentleman of the Bedchamber to the duke. He was one of the few survivors from the Cromwellian attack on Drogheda in 1649. Later he was interrogated in London by Cromwell himself and imprisoned, but managed to ply his guards with drink and escape by a home-made rope to a boat in the Thames and thence get across the Channel where he made his way to the Royalist headquarters in the Low Countries and joined the army.

It was Talbot's marriage which brought him to the fore in Irish affairs and in matters at court. He married Katherine Boynton, who seems to have been a second choice, as his first love, the attractive Frances Jennings, sister-in-law to John Churchill, later Duke of Marlborough, married George Hamilton, an army officer. The two did not meet again for several years when both were single again as George Hamilton died in battle and Katherine died in 1678 and is buried in Christchurch Cathedral, Dublin. In 1681 Frances and Richard married and, both devout Catholics, they settled in London and Dublin, very much in the Duke of York's pay.

Thus it was not surprising that Tyrconnell. as he became, should be made Lord Deputy of Ireland in 1685 when James came to the throne in place of the Earl of Clarendon, a Protestant and moderate. His instructions were laid down in great detail by Sunderland, First Minister to the new king. He was to see that all officers and soldiers of the army in Ireland had to take an oath to the new king, and be dismissed if they refused. Catholic families who had been forced to give up arms in the light of evidence from Titus Oates, had to have them restored, and that positions of sheriffs, justices of the peace, etc. should be open to Catholics. Thus there was no mention that Protestants had to be persecuted or deprived of their jobs, estate or money, but Tyrconnell took it upon himself to build up the Irish civil service as well as the army with loyal Catholics, and he reported at length to his king in January 1689. He had seen the results of the Revolution in England and was concerned that the City of London had voted £300,000 to William for the reduction of Ireland and even more concerned that troops were marching to Chester, Liverpool and Bristol which must mean that Ireland was soon to be invaded.

It is worth quoting large chunks of his report in full as they clearly indicate to us the work he was doing in Ireland, how poor it was and of the great difficulties he was in. [J]:*

> 1. *Your Majesty's kingdom* of Ireland is divided into 4 provinces, viz: Leinster, Munster, Connaught, and Ulster. The catholics in the city of Dublin in Leinster may be guessed to equal in numbers all other religions there (not including soldiers who are all catholics). The catholics in the rest of that Province are 40 to one of all other persuasions. In the Province of Connaught the catholics are 200 to one of all other persuasions. The

★ See *Notes on Sources* pp 151–2

catholics of Ulster are not so considerable, by reason of the greater number of Scotch presbyterians there, yet may be thought to be as many as all the rest . . . all the catholics are most zealously affected to your majesty's service, but amongst the protestants, generally tainted [acquainted?] with the principles of England, there are not in the whole kingdom one hundred that may be relied on to serve your majesty.

2. *The Army*. There are 4 regiments of Old Troopes and one Battalion of the regiment of guards and 3 regiments of horse with one Troop of Grenadiers on Horseback.

I have lately given out commissions for neare 40 regiments of foot, 4 regiments of dragoons, and two of horse, all of which amounts to near 40,000 men, who are all uncloathed [without uniform] and the greatest part unarmed, and are to be subsisted by their several officers until the last of February next out of their own purses, to the ruin of most of them; but after that day I see no possibility for arming them, clothing them or subsisting them for the future but abandoning the Country to them; but after all if I may be supplied by the last of March with those succours that are necessary which I press in my letter, I doubt not but I shall preserve this Kingdom entirely for your Majesty. [A list of forts and harbours appeared here.]

3. The present state of the revenue is humbly represented to your majesty in the paper hereto annexed.

4. I have already sent my Lord Mountjoy and Lord Chief Baron Rice to your majesty who will inform you at large of all our wants, and what you may supply us.

5. I will obey your Majesty in that article [presumably that if no money is forthcoming he will allow the unpaid troops to ravage the countryside].

6. As to your Protestant subjects the most considerable of them [about 1500 left for England] as well as Peers as Commons are now in England, soliciting the Prince of Orange to invade this Kingdom, many of them having taken commission from him and have sent his commissions to several Protestants here. That the Lord Kingston, Lord Mount Alexander, Lord Blany with several other adherents are now in actual rebellion in the county of Sligo and several other parts of Ulster. That knowing your Majesty's pious care of protestants . . . and have been very tender of them, and have of late by proclamation assured those in rebellion of free pardon if they forthwith return to their allegiance, to which I fear at this juncture they will be hardly persuaded.

[Items 7 and 9 say he will do what his majesty instructs].

8. I have raised 35 or 36,000 men (so only 4,000 are equipped with arms and clothing), but without arms to defend them, cloaths to cloath them or money to subsist them, or any visible way to maintaine them unless by letting them live on the spoile of the People, which in six months time will destroy both nation and army.

Tyrconnell

Addition

To advance before the middle of March next at farthest 500,000 crowns in cash, which with our own industry shall serve us for a year.

To send me beside the 8,000 firearms already sent (some had just arrived from France) 6,000 matchlocks more and 6,000 firelocks.

To send me att least 1,200 swords.

To send me 2,000 Carbines and as many pistols and holsters.

To send me a good number of officers to traine.

Tyrconnell must have then retired to his quarters for a few glasses of good wine or Irish brandy. He then scribbles a further addition on the letter before it is despatched. Amongst other things he suggests (quite sensibly):

Wee cannot live without 3 or 4 Light Frigatts upon this Coast which I will find all sorts of Provision for, but Mony I have none for them, nor for the French Officers they shall send us from thence. Let them be advanced 6 months pay. Remember Sir [no longer 'Your Majesty'] 500,000 crowns in mony must be sent and all things else in the Memoire and that Delay is Destruction to this Kingdom and that the 2000,000 Livres a Month which you are allowed there applied to this Kingdom will support your Selfe and it against all yr. Enemies. A good lieut.Gen. for the foot and a good Majr.Gen, must be sent, Sir.

At first both Tyrconnell and more especially James himself had thought of Ireland as a stepping stone to get over to Scotland to help Dundee and thence to England, where James was convinced he still had friends. Sarsfield and other Irish officers were obviously keen that the land question in Ireland should be sorted out first and that James should consider himself King of Ireland rather than worry about his former subjects in Scotland and England. As a result a mere 200 men were sent to help Dundee in Scotland and though they fought well at Killiecrankie they were not enough to win the day at Dunkeld.

Strangely, the French naval commanders never seemed to think that a few frigates based in Dublin Bay would keep off the Williamite transports. It was such an obvious suggestion that the ex-naval James would have suggested it to Louis himself and yet it was ignored and William's army at no time had problems in crossing the Irish channel. When James arrived in person he brought troops, arms but no money. The two Frenchmen Louis trusted – D'Avaux and Maumont – were both entrusted with French livres (Maumont was given 300,000 and D'Avaux 500,000 secretly and told to look after them and keep most for emergencies). The Irish troops were never properly paid and had to live on brass money which rapidly became valueless. Nevertheless Tyrconnell was moved to write to Queen Mary* at St Germains for more brass to be sent over.

When King James finally arrived in March 1689 at Kinsale, Tyrconnell was made a duke. With James's fleet came the Count D'Avaux, French Ambassador, Lord Melfort, James's scheming Scottish secretary, his two illegitimate sons the Duke of Berwick and Henry Fitzjames, both competent soldiers, two hundred other officers both English and Irish including Patrick Sarsfield and the Compte de Rosen, a French lieutenant general with a reputation as a 'hard man' as well as two other lieutenant generals: Maumont and Pusignan. The Marquis de Pontis was an artillery officer and engineer, whose main contribution in Ireland seems to have been the construction of the barrier over the river and Londonderry. Poor Maumont was killed in the siege and Rosen, after threatening to kill Protestant hostages if the besieged inside the town did not give up, was hastened back to France.

There was much argument amongst James's chief supporters. They all disliked Melfort, who was aware of his unpopularity and begged James to send him back to France. James was aware of the need for more troops and arms and having not heard from his first messenger, Lord Dover, as to the French reinforcements, sent Melfort as a back-up to Versailles to find out when these men would arrive. It was a sensible move and both Tyrconnell and D'Avaux could concentrate on fighting the war.

Meanwhile in England William was putting his army on a war footing. The twenty thousand men that made up Marshal Schomberg's army were mostly Dutch regulars and Huguenots along with some English recruits. The 73-year-old Marshal, who had led his invasion army in 1668 without having to fight a battle, was supported by General Solms, senior Dutch officer, and the naval squadron of Admiral Rooke. With support from the Ulster Protestants, Schomberg had four cavalry regiments, one dragoon regiment and eighteen infantry, most of which had seen no action before.

There were no Irish troops present to stop Marshal Schomberg's invasion in August. Tyrconnell was ill and the French General, Rosen,

---

* James' queen, Mary of Modena, had great influence in the French Court.

was occupied with collecting together the Irish army that had suffered defeat at both Londonderry and at Newtown Butler, so Schomberg had a free hand. The fact that he spent two weeks taking Carrickfergus and effectually defeated himself by his army suffering from sickness at Dundalk, helped prolong the struggle, but it also meant that William's arrival with a huge army the following year was inevitable.

The French attitude needs careful examination at this stage as it seems that Louis was unduly influenced by Louvois, his minister of war. The arrival of James and his queen and their baby son at the French court in December 1688 was a shock to Louis but he had responded with the utmost courtesy. In fact it is said even the road from Boulogne to Paris had been improved so as not to upset the queen's carriage. A palace was set aside for them and their entourage and all sorts of courtly pleasantries including a chest of money for the queen were provided. [H]

In spite of this, Louis was reluctant to commit too many French troops to Ireland. His minister Louvois, whom James calls great and powerful, was even more reluctant to supply troops that were needed in the Netherlands, Savoy and on the Spanish frontier on such risky business. They could not have been too impressed with the messages from Melfort, D'Avaux and others. The six thousand French troops which were eventually sent to Kinsale in March 1690 under the Comte de Lauzun were only lent from the Savoy front in exchange for Mountcashel's brigade of just under six thousand Irish soldiers, poorly dressed and equipped but eventually to prove very useful soldiers. It was a strange deal. The personality of Lauzun has to be considered in detail. He was described as ambitious, malicious, unscrupulous, a gambler, lacking in charm, and, according to the Duke of Berwick, 'so long (since) he has been in the army that he must have forgot much of the method of war.'

The French General St Ruth, who was eventually to command the Jacobite army at Aughrim, was by far the most competent Jacobite leader to fight in Ireland. Louis must have known this so why wasn't St Ruth sent at this stage instead of the incompetent Lauzun? The pleas of King James for Lauzun can be explained as it was Lauzun who had rescued his queen and son from William's grasp and successfully conveyed them to France. The two men were about the same age and had known each other for some time. The queen naturally thought the world of him. Louis had at one time imprisoned him and Louvois disliked him. Perhaps they wanted him out of the country? At any rate he was made captain general, given both D'Avaux, who was now back in France, and Rosen's jobs together with instructions to safeguard his troops and bring them all back safely. The French war office wanted to keep William's army busy in Ireland so that he could not reinforce the army in the Netherlands. The fact that Louvois was so stingy with arms and equipment – many of the muskets were unusable – was possibly in his nature or that he didn't expect to see them again. He knew Schomberg's abilities as a general and guessed that any battle would be won easily by a general of vast experience as against a king and courtier with a semi-trained, poorly equipped Irish army that, so far, had nothing to show for itself at all. The loss of Londonderry in July 1689 was not something that the French could feel happy about and not even the French naval victory at Bantry Bay* was seen as a reason for celebration, although Herbert had been chased out of the harbour. Seignelai, French Minister of Marine, wrote to Admiral Château-Renault saying he might have done better, which was probably what William thought of Herbert, whom he nevertheless created Earl of Torrington, because half a victory at this stage was better than none at all and Herbert had at least been successful in getting his army safely to Torbay.

Tyrconnell, recovered from an illness, had been busy building up the Irish army. In March he had a letter from the queen in France, who was naturally worried about her husband.

> This is my third letter since I heard from you but shall not make it a long one, for the bearer of it knows a great deal of my mind [Lord Dover], or rather all the thoughts of my heart, for I was so overjoyed to meet with one I durst speak freely to that I opened my heart to him and said more than I am like to do again in haste to anybody. I therefore refer myself to him to tell you all we speak of, for I have no secrets from you; one thing only I must beg of you, to have a good care of the king, and not let him be encouraged by the good news he will hear, for I dread nothing at this time but his going too fast into England, and in manner disadvantageous to those of our persuasion [Catholics] . . . Pray put him often in mynd of being careful of his person, if not for his own sake, for mine, my son's and all our friends are undone if anything amiss happens to him. I dare not let myself go upon this subject I am too full of it, and therefore I need say the less to you, but cannot end my letter without telling you that I never in my life had a truer nor a more sincere friendship for anybody than I have for you. M.R. [J]

It was no wonder that after a letter like this, Tyrconnell should want the king to return to France. Lauzun agreed with him here and this may have been the reason for James's hurried return to France after the Boyne. The queen's letter certainly struck home with Tyrconnell. A live king in safety

* Bantry Bay was a drawn sea battle between the French and Williamites on 1 May, 1689. See Chapter 5 for further details.

one can fight for, but a dead one would be the end of the affair. The same principle Torrington applied to his fleet, that a fleet in being was still a fleet that could fight, so a king in being was still a king whom men could fight for. The queen was certainly right, even if over-emotional, in her appeal to Tyrconnell. He loved his king as much as he loved Ireland. The one he could save, the other he was now becoming too old and tired to do much about. The army could not stop William's army from landing at Carrickfergus on 14 June. James's stores and guns were still in Cork waiting for transport and only eighteen thousand men were ready in the field to fight.

It was, of course, in the French interest that William's army should leave England and get safely into Ireland. This was probably why no French fleet attempted to stop them. Château-Renault had successfully kept open the ports of Cork and Kinsale, which, in the case of Kinsale, was difficult to approach by sail due to the varied winds, angled approach, tide and mud-banks; when there it offered only a completely unwalled port, in spite of two adjacent forts. It was soon seen by the army council in England that if they could not stop the French by sea they could stop them using these ports by land.

Before discussing the Boyne and Aughrim, it is time to look at military tactics and equipment, pay and conditions in both armies.

3

The Commanders and Military Tactics

William's principal commander, Marshal Schomberg, was an experienced campaigner. Seventy-four years old at the time of the Boyne, Hermann was the son of Hans von Schomberg, a diplomat and colonel, who had fought for both the Elector of Brandenburg and the Elector Palatinate. His mother, Anne Sutton, was the daughter of the ninth Lord Dudley and when both his parents died, his mother at his birth and his father a few months later, Hermann was left an orphan. His Dutch grandmother brought him up in Holland and in 1625 he went to the academy at Sedan, followed by Leiden University before entering the army of Frederick Henry of Orange in 1633. He joined the Swedish army the following year and took part in the Battle of Nordlingen, where Ferdinand of Hungary beat a combined force of Swedes and Germans under Count Horne, who was killed in the action, which was an overwhelming victory to Ferdinand.

In 1635 the young Schomberg purchased a company in the army of France, where he became a useful liaison officer as he could speak so many languages. In 1638 he married and took possession of his family property in Geisenheim, transferring back to the Dutch army. William II of Orange made him a Gentleman of the Bedchamber. He became a Calvinist and had to leave the United Provinces in a hurry when he was involved in William's attempt to take Amsterdam in 1650. Thus once more he was back in France where he attracted the attention of Mazarin. In 1652 he became a maréchal-de-camp and served under Turenne. In 1659 he was persuaded to enter the Portuguese army, where he found British troops on his side and was commander of a mixed force against the Spaniards (Louis was anxious to keep Spain busy at home rather than sending troops to defend Holland). Two victories against Spain followed at Almeixal and Montes Claros which guaranteed Portugal her independence from Spain; for the first time Hermann became colonel of a British brigade and in 1673 he was appointed commander of the expeditionary force to capture Walcheren. He had purchased a house at Coubert in France as his wife had died at Geisenheim. He then became a naturalised Frenchman and married a Huguenot lady in 1669. The Walcheren expedition did not materialise so Hermann looked to Louis

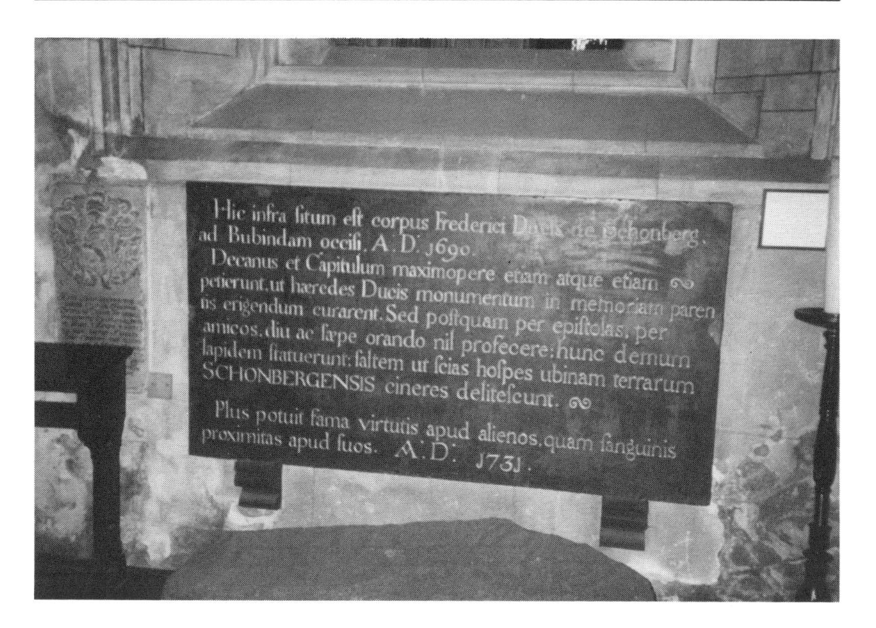

Monument to Marshal Schomberg at St Peter's Cathedral, Dublin

for his next appointment, which was commander of the army on the Sambre and Meuse. In 1674 he was moved to command the small French force fighting Spain in Catalonia. In 1675 Turenne was killed by a cannon ball and Schomberg took over as marshal of the army in Flanders.

However, it was not safe to be married to a Huguenot and to be a Calvinist in France. In 1685 after the Revocation of the Edict of Nantes, he was given permission to return with his family to Portugal. Unemployment did not suit Hermann and he was soon on the move again to Holland, where he met the young William III. He then visited Berlin where the Elector Frederick William made him general-in-chief of the Brandenburg army. Here he became a focus for the fleeing Huguenots. He took a German army into Cologne to forestall French intervention, and thereby ruined his French connections, having his estate in France confiscated and his pension from Portugal cut off.

Once more Hermann was forced to go where he could find both work and money. This time it was back to William, who appointed him general of his Torbay invasion force. He was granted a sum of £100,000 from the English parliament and made a duke. Perhaps he should have now retired and taken up landscape gardening. However, he was persuaded to take on the position of commander of the Irish force of 1689. It was a mistake; his camp at Dundalk was inadequate for the horrendous Irish weather and he had many recruits in his army who were unable to make the basic shelters required. Disease took terrible control of his camp and thousands died. Fortunately the Jacobites who had been threatening the camp drew off in November and Schomberg was able to send his army to winter quarters in the towns and villages of Eastern Ulster. He lost face with William, but the latter did not replace him. In fact he seems to have more or less ignored him. When Schomberg was killed at the Boyne, William does not seem to have been at all put out. Count Meinhard, Schomberg's son, who took a leading role in the Boyne, but was not present at his father's death, has left no record of his feelings but William was unconcerned at the time, as Sir George Clarke says:

> The King immediately had notice of it by one of the Duke's aide-de-Camp, but did not seem to be concerned, whether it was that he really was not sorry or that his thoughts were employed about the regiment of Dutch Guards whom he apprehended in some danger from a body of Irish Horse that was coming to attack them.

Possibly William had never forgiven the Marshal for his dilatoriness at Dundalk but time and again it was only his Dutch commanders whom William felt he could trust. He probably classed Schomberg with those commanders he thought expendable, and in the heat of battle there was no time to weep tears over a lost commander. At least Schomberg's body was taken to Dublin and buried in St Patrick's cathedral where there is a large stone in the duke's memory on one side of the nave. The inscription reads:

> The Dean and Chapter earnestly and repeatedly requested the Duke's heirs to undertake the erection of a monument in memory of their father. It was of no avail. At long last they [the Dean and Chapter] set up this stone. The renown of his valour had greater power among strangers than had the ties of blood among his kith and kin. AD 1731.

The author of this inscription is Dean Swift, famous author of *Gulliver's Travels* and Dean of St Patricks from 1713 to 1745.

The other commanders in William's army were in the Danish contingent of mercenaries and included the German Duke of Wurtemburg, aged thirty-one, who had some experience fighting Swedes and Turks. His commander of cavalry was Colonel de la Forest. His commander of infantry, another German, Julius Ernst Van Tettau was a major-general at the age of forty-six and had served in the Dutch army. He had also been in the French army and had studied fortifications under Turenne, so his services were often in demand not only for sieges but for advice on mining walls or attacking cities. William's chaplain, René de Letablère, was later given a tablet in St Patrick's cathedral. His son Daniel became Dean of Tuam. Other generals used by William were Percy Kirke of Sedgemoor fame, James Douglas and Sir John Lanier. In 1691 he sacked these three and sent them to Holland. In their place he appointed Thomas Tollemache, the Huguenot Marquis de Ruvigny and the Scotsman Hugh Mackay of Killiecrankie fame. The other commander who seems to have achieved more than any of William's other generals put together was the Dutchman, Godard van Ginckel, who came to England with William in 1688 and was given the difficult task of quelling a mutiny in a Scottish regiment. Then in 1691, at the age of forty-seven, he was given overall command of William's troops in Ireland. He was to prove a great success and deserved to be made Earl of Athlone. He died at Utrecht in 1703 and I have been unable to find a memorial to him. In Het Loo Palace near Appeldoorn is a ring on display given to him by Queen Mary for his victory at Aughrim and Limerick. One wonders if he ever wore it.

On James's side the generals were very mixed. The French sent General Rosen originally, but James sent him back after he had behaved in a very unchivalrous way at the Siege of Londonderry. Rosen, frustrated with the lack of progress during the siege, rounded up local Protestants and threatened to kill them unless the defenders opened up their gates. However the leaders in Londonderry erected a gibbet and threatened to kill their Jacobite captives. Richard Hamilton intervened, sent the captives home and Rosen was dismissed. The Irish officers did not always get on with the French leaders, but all seemed to like the Marquis St Ruth, who was the most efficient and competent of James's generals. Lauzun was a courtier and not a general, and Berwick, James's natural son, was a young man, barely twenty at the time of the Boyne. Patrick Sarsfield, later Earl of Lucan, was an enigma for he took virtually no part in the Battle of the Boyne, was only concerned with the end of Aughrim and was largely famous for the Ballyneety raid on William's artillery.

There was one other very competent French commander, the Marquis de Boisseleau, who commanded the garrison in Limerick during the first siege. He understood Irish troops and he was respected by them. Macaulay, the nineteenth century historian, says that the French 'were as much out of the pale of the civilized world as if they had been banished to Dahomey or Spitzbergen. The climate affected their health and spirits. In that unhappy country, wasted by years of predatory war, hospitality could offer little more than a couch of straw, a trencher of meat half raw and half burned, and a draught of sour milk.' The Irish officers though looked after themselves.

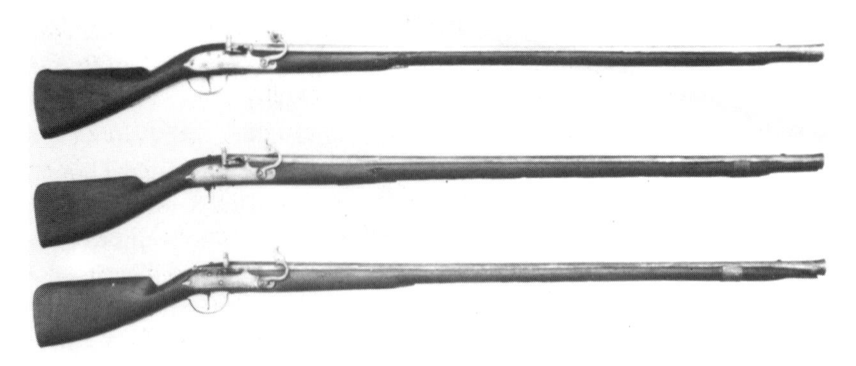

Matchlock muskets of the late 17th century. The bottom one is supposed to have been used at the Boyne

Lord Kilmallock, when promoted to command a Jacobite cavalry regiment in 1691, took with him three horses and his wife fixed him up with: 'A tent, six chairs and stools, five pewter dishes, a dozen plates, a frying pan and a pot with a cover, enabling him to campaign in modest style.' [L]

The miracle was that the French fought as well as they did and that in William's army so many different nationalities got on with each other. Communications for both armies were always difficult but seemed to be overcome. The differences in style of action must now be considered.

The tactics in both William's and James's armies had changed in many ways from those used by the two armies in the Civil War and by Cromwell's troops in Ireland. The pikeman had almost disappeared, the musket had become much lighter and the bayonet appeared for the first time. The English troops at Killiekrankie suffered because they could not fire their muskets with their clumsy plug bayonets, but ring and socket bayonets were soon introduced though there were few around at the Boyne. Some of William's soldiers were described as 'screwing their swords to their muskets'.

The Jacobites used matchlocks, which meant they had to carry a lighted match to fire them and in the Irish rain this must have been a problem. Many of William's troops had firelocks or the more expensive snaphaunce flintlocks. The snaphaunce or fusile was much lighter than the old musket or matchlock. It was fired from the shoulder, and had double the rate of fire. Of a smaller calibre, it fired sixteen balls per pound of lead rather than twelve, and the cartridge was made of paper with the round and correct amount of black powder inserted, so loading and firing was much quicker. King James had a special fusilier regiment to guard the ammunition waggons to save sudden explosions.

Sentries on duty were provided with a flintlock so as not to give away their positions. In battle the musketeers fought in six ranks with the pikemen drawn up behind, unless there was a cavalry charge, when they stood in front. The first rank of musketeers crouched, the second knelt and the third stood up so that one could let off a volley and then file to the back so that the other ranks would fire while they reloaded their muskets. This required a great deal of training and some regiments (a regiment was about 250–300 men) were far more experienced than others. Men were enrolled by their colonels, who were expected to pay for their first wages and uniforms. Thus colonels were usually wealthy landowners and often titled members of the aristocracy.

The cavalry were armed with swords, pistols and carbines (short muskets). They charged with swords using the weight of their horses to break up infantry. The caracole, a military manœuvre when horsemen approached, fired pistols and carbines and withdrew, had largely vanished. Sarsfield was a particularly successful cavalry leader who had started his career as a lieutenant in Lord Dover's Fourth Troop of Horse Guards.

In 1688 his fellow officers were as follows:

Henry, Lord Dover	–	Captain (Jacobite)
Richard, Lord Colchester	–	Lieutenant (Williamite)
Lord C. Hamilton	–	Cornet
James Griffin	–	Guidon (Jacobite)
Henry Margan	–	Quarter Master (Williamite)
Mike Steddons, George Blount, John Tompkins, Ambrose Cave	–	brigadiers and all Jacobites except Ambrose who deserted to William's army at Salisbury
Dr William Starkey	–	Chaplain
Pierre Coudray	–	Surgeon

(A brigadier was a squadron commander and not a brigadier as in today's army.)

Thus not only were tactics used by both sides of great similarity, but whole regiments split into two in 1688, some siding with William, some escaping to France to join James. Lord Colchester managed to take sixty men with him to join William while Sarsfield with some friends made their way to France and from there to Ireland.

A cavalry regiment that fought for William with distinction, Colonel Wynne's horse from Enniskillen, called by William his 'Inniskilling

Horse' have been aptly described by Story* who saw them at the time of the Boyne. They numbered eight troops of fifty men.

> Three regiments of volunteer irregulars, some on big horses, some on small, some furnished with a very fair imitation of a regular trooper's equipment, others with nothing military but their arms; some had holsters, while others carried pistols stuck into their belts, and the majority of the privates had their servants riding behind them on small country ponies called garrons.

These men captured Tyrconnell's carriages at the Boyne and captured £1,000 in money and plate. They also fought well at Aughrim. No doubt some of the captured money was used to buy saddles and equipment for their regiments.

There were two other types of mounted soldiers that were not very common in the Civil War – dragoons and mounted grenadiers. The dragoons were mounted infantry with pistols, carbines or muskets and some had halberds. They fought on foot as did the Irish dragoon commander Sir Neil O'Neill at the Boyne, covering a ford for an hour and stopping an enemy advance. They could usually carry more ammunition than the ordinary musketeer and could advance and retire rapidly. They tended to be on the wings of the army in battle so that they could prevent encirclement. In the Civil War Okey's musketeers at Naseby had fought behind a hedge but Prince Rupert's cavalry had passed on either side of them so that their fire had been ineffective. This would not happen with the dragoons, who could use their halberds as pikes if necessary and take up positions of strength on a small hill or in a ruined building.

The mounted grenadier carried a grenade made from a hollow iron sphere filled with gunpowder and plugged with a wooden stopper. In this was a length of match that had to be ignited. They threw this into defended positions and were often tall men. The grenadiers also fought on foot and John Evelyn describes them in 1678 as he went to see the army at Hounslow Heath.

> The whole army in Battalia, a very glorious sight: now were brought into service a new sort of soldier called *Granadiers*, who were dextrous to fling granados, every one having a pouch full, and had furred caps with coped crowns like Janizaries, which made them look very fierce, and some had

* The Rev. George Story was an English army chaplain who accompanied William's army. His two works *A true and impartial history* . . . 1691 and *A continuation of the impartial history of the wars in Ireland*, 1693 are quoted in *The Irish Sword* Vol XVIII, No. 70.

long hoods hanging down behind as we picture fools: their clothing being likewise pybald yellow and red.

We shall see how Tiffin's grenadiers at the second siege of Limerick led the attack and how other grenadiers at the first siege got into the city but had to retire as they had not been properly supported by infantry.

The artillery was almost an unused arm in the field for James as he strangely sent off his guns and baggage before the Boyne to Dublin as if anticipating defeat. His French colleagues had some manoeuvrable 6-pounders, one of which nearly accounted for William himself. The Williamite forces had a proper train of artillery, which was sent to Ireland by the king and carefully detailed by the Tower of London records, consisting of the following personnel:

5	Engineers		
2	Gentlemen of the Ordnance		
12	Conductors for Waggons		
2	Master Carpenters		
14	Carpenters		
2	Master Wheelwrights		
6	Wheelwrights		
1	Master Smyth		
6	Smyths		
1	Master Tynman		
6	Tynmen		
1	Asst. for Tyn Boates		
1	Another asst. for Tyn Boates		
1	Master Surgeon		
4	Asst. Surgeons		
100	Waggoners		
1	Master Gunsmith		
19	Gunsmiths	Total Cost:	£77.14s.5d
24	Gunners	plus looping for 900 horses:	£56. 5s.0d
208		30 Matrosses (Fusiliers employed as)	£1.10s. 0d
30		Incidental Charge:	£5.0s.0d
Total: 238			£140.9s.5d

The matrosses were assistants who were responsible for loading and unloading the guns, sighting them for the gunners to fire. They also had to clean the barrels and sometimes naval personnel were used for this job as they had more experience. The waggoners, who travelled with their families, moved at a slow pace and not only the heavy guns had to be drawn by the horses, but also the twenty 'tyn boates', presumably on waggons, had their special personnel with a Master Tynman in charge. Pontoons had been used by the New Model Army at the Battle of Worcester but these 'tyn boates' were a new idea and presumably, when constructed, a pontoon bridge remained in place for a long time so if it had a tin bottom it might last even longer.

Both armies made use of scouts, which were often dragoons or squadrons of cavalry. The Irish used rapparees for information and extra horses, but these people, rather like the clubmen of England during the Civil War, were independent and were out for themselves not for either of the participants.

Supplies were the responsibility of the quartermasters. When Schomberg arrived in Ireland he had no waggons or horses and the English fleet used Carrickfergus as their main depot. In September 1689 Schomberg complained to Lord Portland that he could not advance due to lack of bread. John Shales, the Commissary-General, was blamed but the real culprit was a Mr Harbord, purveyor and pay-master of the forces in Ireland. Horses en route for the army had been sold to farmers in the Wirral, salt and meat had slipped through the net and been sold for the benefit of Mr Harbord and when the latter was finally arrested in 1690 there was a deficit of £406,000.* Shales was made the scapegoat and dismissed and two men were appointed by the House of Commons, William Robinson and Bartholomew Vanhomright, who went to Ireland as replacement commissary-generals.

William gave the contract for bread supply to a civilian contractor, Isaac Pereira, whose firm was based in The Hague, to supply no less than thirty six thousand 1½lb loaves to the army every day for the sum of 1/¼d a loaf. The paymaster stopped this amount from every soldier per day and paid Pereira quarterly. The system seemed to work. A base hospital was made in Dublin after the Boyne and a field hospital accompanied the army on the march although there was not much faith in regimental surgeons.

The ships used by the Williamite forces were mostly Whitehaven colliers – eighteen were made into troop transports and twenty-nine into horse transports.

The French used Kinsale and Cork as their main ports of entry but switched to Galway and Limerick, in spite of their distance up river, after

* A bed and meal for the night in 1690 cost 3d for a common soldier. Today it might cost £15. If this is correct then the sum of £406,000 would be the modern equivalent of many millions of pounds.

Marlborough's capture of the southern ports. James did not make use of the French fleet to supply and fortify Dublin's port at Dun Laoghaire. The Jacobites however did have a waggon train of 170 waggons, 400 carts and ten gun carriages by 1691. They also used pack horses and men and women carrying back-baskets.

At sieges both sides made use of fascines made from brushwood and bundles of wool. The British infantry at Aughrim used wooden hurdles to get over the bog. This and pontoon bridges on tin pontoons were innovations of almost twentieth-century importance. Henceforward a river was no protection for an army and there were few cases of men being drowned by accident.

The Dutch troops carried a *chevaux de frise*, a sort of portable fence, the sticks of which were carried by infantrymen, that kept out horses. It was remarkably effective but the Huguenots at the Boyne did not have such a thing so their infantry was made to suffer by the Irish horse.

TACTICAL AIMS: LONDONDERRY AND NEWTOWN BUTLER

The first aim of James's and Tyrconnell's Irish army was to capture Northern Ireland for their cause. Tyrconnell wanted Jacobite control of the whole army. James, when he arrived, saw the country as a stepping stone to recapture Scotland and then England, but he realised that Ireland must be settled first. Ulster was controlled by groups of armed Protestants at Hillsborough, Sligo, Enniskillen and Londonderry. In March 1689 General Richard Hamilton set out from Dublin with a small army to attack Sir Arthur Rawdon at Hillsborough. He caught him at Dromore and after a minor skirmish, the Protestants scattered leaving Hillsborough to Hamilton. The arrival of James and Count Rosen gave Hamilton's successful little force added strength but caused some confusion in its command structure. Although Sarsfield, given a free 'roaming' hand, made a successful attack on Sligo.

James's army made slow progress to Ulster to put down the Protestants in Enniskillen and Londonderry. In command at the walled city of Londonderry was Robert Lundy, a Scottish colonel from Mountjoy's regiment. Lundy was a timid man, anxious to avoid bloodshed and suggested a surrender but was over-ruled by the citizens, who appointed George Walker, a clergyman, and Major Baker as joint governors. The fiery spirit behind the defence of Londonderry though was Captain Adam Murray, who led a successful sally in April. In this the Jacobites lost two of their officers and Richard Hamilton who commanded their army, was frequently hard pressed to keep the siege going. Lundy managed to escape from the city disguised as a porter. Was he a traitor or merely an officer trying to keep the peace? History seems to brand him a traitor but, although he was shut in the Tower when he fled to London, he was released as there was no definite proof of his guilt.

The Jacobites built a boom across the River Foyle to stop boats attempting to relieve the garrison, which after three months was desperately short of supplies. People inside the town were reduced to eating dogs and cats, dysentery was rife, and yet the relieving force was within sight but nothing seemed to be happening. Colonel Kirke, now promoted to general, was in command of the relieving force. He had spent some time at the Isle of Man due to contrary wind and bad weather and only approached the city at the end of July. *HMS Mountjoy* rammed the boom, failed to break it and ran aground. A longboat with sailors tried to cut it and finally the *Mountjoy* and the *Phoenix* braved the Jacobite guns, suffering some casualties including the captain of the *Mountjoy*, before reaching the city at night and unloading their valuable cargoes of biscuit and beef, with sacks of flour, peas and oatmeal. The unloading went on all night while Kirke's squadron bombarded the Jacobite gun positions. Next morning the flashing of the bayonets showed the Jacobite army marching away. The siege was over. It was 1 August and it had lasted 105 days. Some 3,000 men including Governor Baker died, mostly of sickness, and at least 8,000 of the Jacobite forces, many of whom had to live in terrible conditions round the town.

The morale of the Jacobite army decreased rapidly after the Londonderry disaster. The Irish blamed the French officers and vice-versa, although all were glad to get back to reasonable quarters after living in the wet trenches round Londonderry. James and his advisors had by now realised that their present army was not strong enough to capture Ireland, and at least they had learnt that they were no good at besieging towns – but defending them against enemy besiegers might be another matter as William was soon to discover.

The 27 July saw the Battle of Killicrankie in Scotland, and two days later the defenders of Enniskillen fought the Battle of Newtown Butler. Situated at the junction of Lough Erne and Upper Lough Erne, the town folk had the island, surrounded by a ditch and connected by a bridge to the town in which to defend themselves, but it was unsatisfactory. They appealed to Kirke for help, and he sent them some muskets and ammunition and a few officers, including a Staffordshire man, Colonel Wolseley. They arrived in a ship which was eagerly welcomed by the population. Wolseley was an inspired choice. He had been responsible for tossing the pro-Jacobite Mayor of Scarborough in a blanket after the man had made an address in favour of James II when William had landed at Torbay.

Meanwhile, General Macarthy, whom James created Viscount Mountcashel, was pushing up from Clones towards Enniskillen. Crum Castle was besieged and Lieutenant Colonel Berry, Wolseley's second-in-command, who had been sent on ahead was forced to flee pursued by Anthony Hamilton's dragoons. Wolseley was outnumbered and had no field guns but his men were in good spirits. Mountcashel took up a position on a slight rise near the village of Newtown Butler. His front was protected by a bog with only a causeway across it and this he faced with his small cannon. The Enniskillen infantry charged over the causeway and killed the gunners. Then their horse charged over – no longer scared of being shot down. The dragoons, it is alleged, received the wrong command and retired with Hamilton in the lead. Mountcashel did his best, but most of his infantry and he himself were surrounded and captured. His cavalry and many of his infantry who fled were killed or drowned trying to cross Lough Erne. This was a significant victory which gave the town folk of Enniskillen time to recover and, persuaded James after he had escaped, to send Mountcashel and his regiment to France in the ships which brought him, Count Lauzun and the French army that fought at the Boyne. Strangely the Jacobites were faced with the same sort of defensive problem at Aughrim with a causeway to defend. This time they used a castle in which to put their guns and had dragoons and cavalry handy to stop the enemy's advance. We shall see how they managed.

It was no small achievement of King William to get a large army and its horses, supplies, cannon etc. from the camp on Hounslow Heath to Chester. Fifteen thousand men had to get over the Irish Sea. According to the *London Gazette* his route was from Hounslow to Northampton on a Wednesday in early June 1690, Northampton to Lichfield on the Thursday, Lichfield to Whitchurch, Shropshire on Friday and Whitchurch to Colonel Whitley's house (where William spent the night) between Chester and Hoylake. The route was about 290 miles in length.

The train of three thousand ox-carts stretched for at least eighteen miles and these were just the supplies, tents, ammunition, etc. and there must have been a cavalry detachment ahead clearing the road. One waggon breaking down would have held everything up and the road, especially round Whitchurch is very narrow, even today, so anything coming in the other direction would need to be directed off the road quickly. The route takes some of the A5 road today and would have had the benefit of John Ogilby's road map. The road north from Northampton would through Brington, Long Buckby, Watford Gap, Kilsby, Hillmorton, Rugby, Coventry and then north to Lichfield.

The dust would have been tremendous on a hot day. Steep hills would have been a problem, not so much as climbing them but going down, the waggoners would have to apply their primitive brakes made of wedges. Very steep hills sometimes had to be negotiated backwards, or with men with supporting ropes for each waggon. It was no wonder that armies moved slowly.

The 6,000 Danes were camped in Hull, still a walled town, and they had an easier march over the Pennines to Chester. The English regiments with William were mostly recruits, most had never fought in action before and some had been in James's army so William would have had doubts about them. In the van though were his Dutch guards and his Huguenot troops with whom he had absolute confidence.

HASTINGS REGIMENT

It is worth looking in some detail at one regiment that fought at the Boyne and with Marlborough at Cork and Kinsale. This was Hastings Regiment, which was formed by the Earl of Huntingdon in 1685. There were fifty men in a company and ten companies. Each company had a captain, lieutenant, ensign, two sergeants, three corporals and about fifty men. They also had a drummer boy who kept time on the march. The men were either musketeers, carrying flintlocks, grenadiers who had an axe as well as a musket and at first a few pikemen though these were replaced with muskets with bayonets. They wore red coats, yellow breeches and a sash on which they hung their cartridges. Their grenadiers had a high hat with a tassel, the others hats with brims, one side of which was turned up – rather like the Australian infantry in World War II.

The Captain was paid eight shillings a day, the lieutenant four shillings, the sergeants and corporals three shillings and a soldier only eight pence. A year's wages for the regiment was £10,922.12s.6d., which was why at first it was only wealthy men who could raise a regiment. At the time of William's landing at Torbay, the regiment was at Plymouth Citadel with the Earl of Bath's Foot. The Earl and three officers were put into custody as they were Catholics. So the lieutenant colonel, Ferdinando Hastings, took command. The regiment renamed after their colonel, gave its support to William and in January 1689 four companies went to Leicester, one to Mountsorrel (presumably stationed in the castle there), two to Loughborough and two to Ashby de la Zouche (where the castle had been mostly pulled down after the Civil War, but probably still sufficiently intact to house soldiers). The regiment was highly thought of as it was included in General Mackay's army to suppress the Highlands. Mackay wrote afterwards: 'There was no regiment or troop with me but behaved like the vilest cowards in nature except Hastings (13th) and Lord Leven's (25th) whom I must praise at such a degree as I cannot but blame others.'

However, Colonel Hastings himself was in trouble for equipping his men in some uniforms from another regiment. It seems he took care of his men first and worried about officialdom afterwards. In October, Hastings' Regiment crossed over to Ireland as part of Schomberg's army, landing at Carlingford on 9 October, a two-day voyage from Scotland. Most of William's army embarked at Hoylake on the Wirral, a port now silted up, but convenient as it was only a day's march from Chester.

The regiment went into quarters at Lisburn along with those of Lloyd-Babington, Cutts and Foulkes (who had fought for Monmouth at Sedgemoor and escaped to Holland afterwards), the Danish horse and foot and the Dutch horse. They moved from Lisburn to Armagh in June to await the arrival of William with the main army.

At the Boyne, Hastings' Regiment were not seriously engaged. They were on the right wing facing the French. They don't seem to have been short of numbers after the battle as it is recorded they took part in the march past King William at Dublin's St Patrick's Cathedral on 7 July. The regiment then numbered six hundred and six. Brigadier Trelawney (also a Sedgemoor veteran) was given Hastings' and four other regiments of foot and one of horse to look after Dublin. However, the French success at Beachy Head* and the threat to England , meant reliable troops had to be sent home. Thus the order came to return to Chester at the end of July. They then moved to Abingdon via Worcester and then via Basingstoke and Petersfield to Portsmouth where they relieved the 1st Foot Guards on 15 August. On 25 August the Earl of Nottingham wrote to Marlborough at Portsmouth that:

> Our will and pleasure is that as soon as our fleet shall arrive at Spithead you cause the following Regiments of Foot to embark on board the same viz: the Prince of Denmark's, the regiment commanded by Colonel Charles Trelawney, the Regiment of Fusiliers, the Princess of Denmark's, The Regiments commanded by Col.F.Hastings, Col.Hailes, Sir David Collier, and Colonel Fitzpatrick and that you go on board our fleet and take upon you the command of the said Regiments and sundry other forces as shall be added to them pursuant to such orders and directions from Us

* The French navy won a convincing naval battle against a combined Anglo-Dutch fleet off Beachy Head on 30 June 1690 the day before the Battle of the Boyne. (See Chapter 5 for more details.)

> and for doing this shall be your warrant. Given at our Court at Whitehall this 25th day of August 1690 in the 2nd year of our reign. By Her Majesty's Command, NOTTINGHAM. [E]

The document was headed MARIE R. as Queen Mary in her own right issued the command, although it was set out by Nottingham, her chief minister. This time the regiment did get some action. On the attack of Kinsale in October 1690 they were in the attack on the New Fort. Some men were lost in action but far more suffered from disease. At the end of the action only 462 rank and file were fit for duty out of a contingent of 650.

After wintering in Cork, the regiment was summoned to help the Royal Dragoons, who had been surrounded at Drumaugh. Near Ballycleugh they found Jacobite soldiers lining the hedges. Hastings ordered a charge and fifty opponents were killed and the rest ran off. The Royal Dragoons were rescued. Hastings led his men on to Drummaneer which surrendered. Shortly after this they were sent home.

William's total army which met up in Ireland then consisted of 2,991 horse, 1,270 dragoons, 25,021 foot and 5,500 Danish foot and 800 Danish horse (see Appendix A). The Dutch contingent under Count Solms numbered 2,300 and the Huguenots under Colonel Caillemotte numbered 2,600 of which less than 400 were horse. James's army was about 25,000 but many of his best men were in garrisons like that at Drogheda and took no part in the forthcoming battle (see Appendix C). Tyrconnell had suggested a retreat to beyond the Shannon, some others wanted to burn Dublin but James was anxious to fight. He knew his time was limited and he stopped at the Boyne, where he took up his headquarters at Donore church, his cavalry at Plattin Hall, his foot watching the river and his French allies in the second line.

The stage was set for the biggest battle on Irish soil since 1601 when the Spaniards had been beaten in Kinsale. The Jacobites had only a day to fortify the river bank. La Hougette, one of the French officers present, considered it a good defensive position. Others like Tyrconnell knew the river could have been forded in many places and must have been worried by this.

William's army that camped on the other bank were more confident. There were more of them. They had experienced troops to the fore, experienced leaders, and above all they believed in their king,

The Irish tents, especially those closest to the river, must have had some anxious sleepers that night. The Williamite tents, out of cannon range up on the hill, were better placed and their occupants slept soundly believing in their king. The northern bank of the Boyne is Conyngham country, and the Marquess's home Slane Castle, with its fine woods, borders the river. Their family crest is a unicorn but there is also another one more appropriate for this occasion. It shows an arm encased in armour raised high holding a sword. * The Battle of the Boyne was about to begin and its outcome would decide which king would rule Ireland, which religion would rule Ireland and it would shape the nature of the country politically for the following three hundred years.

* The author used to possess a Coyningham sugar bowl with the unicorn crest but on consulting *Fairbairn's Book of Crests*, the alternative can be seen in Plate 2. No. 8.

4

The Boyne, 1 July 1690

For those who think that the Battle of the Boyne was the Irish against the English, the truth is that William's English regiments were all in the second rank, as reserves, and it was the Dutch, the Huguenots – who were French Protestants, Germans, and others – and the Danes with the men of Enniskillen in the front rank who did most of the fighting. On the Irish side it was the cavalry and the hard-pressed foot, that did not take to their heels, who bore the brunt of the action. The French, apart from organising an orderly retreat and covering it with their guns did little. Like Bosworth Field two hundred years earlier some men just stood and watched.

The Jacobite army, some twenty-five thousand strong, commanded a good position on the banks of the River Boyne within eyeshot of Drogheda, which had been strongly fortified and garrisoned. The bridge at Slane was broken down. James had placed his headquarters at Donore church, where the hill overlooks the river. His foot was down at Oldbridge, his horse in four squadrons at Plattin Hall (near the modern cement works) and his dragoons were a mobile force ready to block any river crossing. His 6pdr guns were also fairly mobile and, as we shall see, nearly won the day before the battle commenced. His troops did not have time to fortify their positions, though the cottages at Oldbridge (where there was a known ford but no bridge) were occupied by his infantry. Tyrconnell and Dominic Sheldon, who commanded the cavalry, were concerned that the river was fordable in several places and that the loop of the river was surrounding the Irish infantry.

William's army marched about fifteen miles from Ardee and arrived on Tullyallen Hill the afternoon of the last day in June. His guns arranged on the hill facing the river soon opened up on Jacobite positions without doing much damage. In fact the ever-curious William decided to move down to the river bank and see the Jacobite positions himself. His horrified officers watched when a party of Jacobite horse in the field opposite waited until William, who had sat on the grass, mounted his horse to ride away. The Rev. Story, who was present, takes up the description of what then happened:

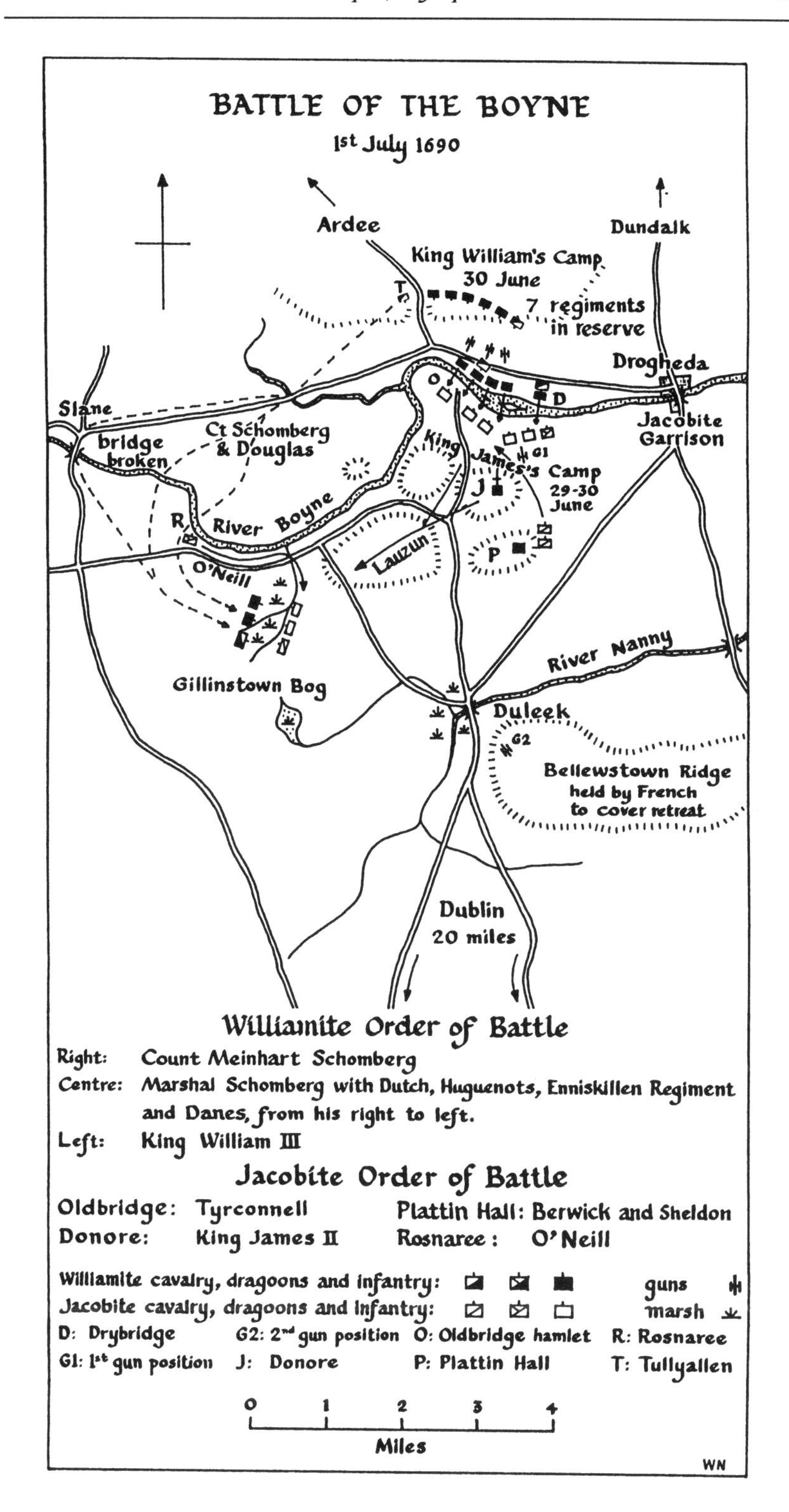
BATTLE OF THE BOYNE
1st July 1690
Ardee
Dundalk
King William's Camp 30 June
7 regiments in reserve
T
Drogheda
D
Jacobite Garrison
Slane
bridge broken
Ct Schomberg & Douglas
O
King James's Camp 29-30 June
G1
J
R
River Boyne
Lauzun
P
O'Neill
River Nanny
Gillinstown Bog
Duleek
G2
Bellewstown Ridge held by French to cover retreat
Dublin 20 miles
Williamite Order of Battle
Right: Count Meinhart Schomberg
Centre: Marshal Schomberg with Dutch, Huguenots, Enniskillen Regiment and Danes, from his right to left.
Left: King William III
Jacobite Order of Battle
Oldbridge: Tyrconnell
Donore: King James II
Plattin Hall: Berwick and Sheldon
Rosnaree: O'Neill
Williamite cavalry, dragoons and infantry:
Jacobite cavalry, dragoons and infantry:
guns
marsh
D: Drybridge
G1: 1st gun position
G2: 2nd gun position
J: Donore
O: Oldbridge hamlet
P: Plattin Hall
R: Rosnaree
T: Tullyallen
0 1 2 3 4
Miles
WN

Battle of the Boyne: Looking north from King James's position

Battle of the Boyne: The banks of the River Boyne, showing the distance William's troops had to cross

> This small party [of Jacobites] brought two field pieces with them, dropping them by a hedge, in the ploughed land undiscovered, they did not offer to fire them until His Majesty was mounted and then, he and the rest riding back softly the same way, their gunner fired a piece which killed us two horses and a man, about a hundred yards above where the King was, but immediately came a second which had almost been a fatal one, for it grazed upon the bank of the river, and in the rising slanted upon the King's right shoulder, took out a piece of coat, and tore the skin and flesh and afterwards broke the head of a gentleman's pistol.[G]

Luckily William was wearing a thick coat, but he lost some blood, and must have fallen from his horse for the Jacobites cheered and the despatch to France said that he had been killed. However, the king called for his cloak to cover the hole in his jacket and rode round his troops with Old Schomberg to the cheers of his men. Had he been killed the battle might have been lost, though there was a natural chain of command and Queen Mary would still have carried on in England as queen in her own right. It must have caused consternation on the Williamite side and, for the Jacobite side, some sort of boost to their fighting spirits. James himself though was not anxious to kill his own son-in-law. To take away his crown was one thing, but to kill him quite another. He must have recalled what had happened to his own father.

That night in the William camp around the ruined Mellifont Abbey which he had made his headquarters, a battle conference was held. The Dutch Count Solms proposed a frontal attack at Oldbridge, which he would lead personally. He was a brave but arrogant man, disliked by the English officers. Marshal Schomberg suggested that a right wing attack led by his son Meinhard and a feint at Oldbridge would separate the Jacobites from the road to Dublin. William listened in silence then proposed a compromise. One third of the army would leave at 5 a.m. the next morning and make for Slane and the ford at Rosenaree. Meinhard would lead the van and Douglas the support when he had word that the fords had been crossed. They already knew Slane bridge had been broken but there was a ford beside it that was passable at low tide. The tide – like the River Parrett in Somerset – made high water time impassable for fords, but at low water, there were about two hours for this. The Williamites knew this and had to plan their attack carefully.

William was in his element. Like so many aristocrats at the time, William had been brought up in the saddle. He was always happy hunting and the same feeling must have come to him as if he was hunting. No doubt the excitement would rub off on his troops. Orders were given that every man should wear a green bough in his hat to distinguish them from Jacobites, who were wearing white cockades made of paper. Schomberg complained that he was more used to giving orders than receiving them. The stage was set for the battle. James, on the other bank, was hampered by the early morning mist so he did not see Meinhard's troops file out early making for Slane. He did however agree with his French commander, the Comte de Lauzun, whose troops were in reserve, that a detachment of dragoons under Neil O'Neill should watch the ford at Rosenaree. This was fortunate indeed though four hundred men against ten thousand could only have a small effect. However this small band of dragoons held up Meinhard for an hour of valuable time.

Macaulay's account of the battle concentrates on Oldbridge and on James's flight. The best accounts are by King James himself and La Hougette, a French officer, as well as the Duke of Berwick's memoirs.

Most of the action took place at Oldbridge. Tyrconnell realised that the only two Irish regiments, that of Lords Antrim and Clanrickarde, were insufficient to guard the hamlets, he moved down five further infantry regiments under Richard Hamilton. Behind them he drew up his cavalry, which had been based at Plattin Hall. These were his own half regiment, Parker's, Sutherland's and Berwick's.

The Williamites waited until midday when the tide was right for crossing, then the Dutch guards waded over, followed by the Huguenots under Caillemote and the Enniskilleners, leaving William and the Danes, Dutch horse, and the English regiments on the northern bank. Here we can quote James's account, most probably dictated to him afterwards by General Dorrington who was with the Jacobite guards. The river was at least thirty yards wide where William crossed.

> As for what pass'd at Old Brig, it seems the enemy perceiving the left wing and most of the foot had marched after Lauzun, attacked the regiment which was at the foot of Old Brig with a great body of foot all strangers, and soon possessed themselves of it; upon which the seven battalions of the first line which were left there and drawn up a little behind the rising ground which sheltered them from the enemy's cannon marched up to charge them, and went on boldly till they came within a pike's length of the enemy notwithstanding their perpetual fire, so that Major Arthur who was at the head of the first battalion of the Guards ran the officer through the body that commanded the battalion he marched up to. But at the same time the enemy's horse began to cross the river [Danes and William] which the King [James] foot perceiving immediately gave way notwithstanding all that Dorrington and the other officers could do to stop them which cost several of the captains their lives as Arundel, Ashton, Dungen,

> Fitzgerald, and two or three more, besides the Marquis de Hoquincourt, who was killed with several others of his brigade. Barker, Lieutenant Colonel of the guards with Arthur the Major were both wounded of which the latter died the same day. [H]

Caillemotte who was in the van with the Huguenot brigade was mortally wounded and carried back over the river, where he died. His men were left leaderless and seeing this, the aged Marshal Schomberg, who was not wearing armour of any kind, dashed across the river and took command. His aides did nothing to stop him. Sir Charles O'Toole, a lieutenant in Dorrington's regiment of Guards, rushed forward with others and cut down the Marshal, who was also shot in the back of the head by a carbine – some say by one of his own men by accident – but it was O'Toole who claimed the deed, though he did not live to see the day out. At the same time the Rev. Walker leading on his Londonderry veterans was killed. The Irish infantry at this stage was fighting fiercely and for half an hour things went well for them.

At the far left wing William had been looking for a ford. Led by Dumont's Huguenot horse, Danish horse and foot, they swarmed over the river in single file. William had brought down two cannon to cover his crossing and also ordered those soldiers waiting to cross, to fire at the enemy on the other bank. Fortunately the enemy only consisted of Dungan's Dragoons, who, on their leader being killed by an early cannon shot from one of the two cannon, mounted their horses and rode off to the rear. William's horse foundered on the mud, two strong Danish soldiers hoisted him out of the water back onto his horse and the contingent crossed in safety. The Irish infantry used up their ammunition, then retreated if they had no more. Everywhere there was the noise of musketry, the scream of men and beasts, the clash of swords and the smoke, which made it difficult to tell friend from foe. The white cockades of the Jacobites could be clearly seen, the yellow coats of the Dutch too but it must have been difficult to see the green badges of William's troops in the hedges and fields; the river battle went on for half an hour before the Williamites gained ground. It was a crucial moment when William went up to the colonel of the Enniskillen troops. At first they didn't recognise him. 'It is his Majesty,' shouted the colonel. 'I have heard much of you,' William replied when the cheering was dying down, 'you shall be my guards, let me see something of you.' No better encouragement could be given to these men from Ulster. They were attacked by the Irish cavalry, lost men, retreated at one point, but, rallied by their king, came on and remained with William until the end. We can now go back to James's account.

> Nevertheless the horse [Irish horse] did their duty with great bravery and tho' they did not break the enemy's foot it was more by reason of the ground's not being favourable than for want of vigour, for after they had been repulsed by the [Williamite] foot they rallied again and charged the enemy's horse [the Enniskillen horse] and beat them every charge. Tyrconnell's and Parker's troops suffered the most on this occasion. [Tyrconnell himself was not fighting with his cavalry]. Powel and Vaudrey, both Lieutenants of the Guards with most of the Exempts [off-duty officers fighting as volunteers] and brigadiers [not senior officers but in the Irish cavalry, juniors] of both troops were slain as also the Earl of Carlingford, Mons. D'Amande and several other volunteers that charged with them. Nugent and Casanone were wounded of Tyrconnell's, Major Mara and Sir Charles Take killed and Captain Bala wounded. Of Parker's the Colonel wounded, the Lieutenant Colonel Green with Dodington the major and many other officers killed and of the two squadrons of that regiment there came but off thirty sound men. Sutherland's regiment, though wounded, suffered not much, having to do only with the enemy's horse which he soon repulsed; in fine they were so roughly handled and overpowered by numbers that at last they were quite broke. Lieut. General Hamilton being wounded and taken prisoner at the last charge, and the Duke of Berwick having his horse shot under him was some time amongst the enemy, he was rid over and ill-bruised; however by the help of a trooper got off again. Sheldon who had commanded the horse had two [horses] killed under him.

The three Hamilton brothers were related to Lady Tyrconnell. Richard, who had been sent over by William from England as an emissary to consult Tyrconnell, had changed sides and been made a Jacobite general. His brother, Anthony, was with the cavalry and had fought without much distinction at Newtown Butler. The third brother, John, fought valiantly at Aughrim and died of wounds in Dublin after that battle.

Meanwhile, on the Jacobite left wing there was a stalemate. James had sent regiments over there, believing this to be the main attack position of William's army. O'Neill's dragoons had extricated themselves and joined up with Lauzun. The land up from Rosnaree is steep and wooded. The area between the two forces – that is Lauzun and Count Schomberg's, had two ditches and a bank. Sarsfield, sent to reconnoitre, said it was totally unsuitable for cavalry. The Count must have realised this too as he pressed on towards the right. James and Lauzun were concerned that the baggage and the guns sent on early in the morning would reach Dublin before the enemy.

A third account now comes into the reckoning. John Stevens was in the Jacobite's Grand Prior's regiment that had been sent forward to help block the Dublin road. His account is of some interest: not because he was involved in the fighting, but because of the aftermath. His regiment, The Grand Prior's, was one of those sent by James to reinforce Sir Neil O'Neill. They never got to grips with the enemy. Instead they were suddenly confronted by the Jacobite cavalry from the Oldbridge direction. Their own horse dashed through their ranks, scattering them, pistols were fired and men took to their heels. There was a general panic and officers like Captain Stevens could do nothing to stop them. Suddenly they were just a rabble.

> What few men I could see I called to, no commands being of force, begging them to stand together and repair to their colours, the danger being in dispersing but all in vain, some throwing away their arms, others even their coats and shoes to run the lighter . . . Only the French can be said to have rallied for only they made head against the enemy and a most honourable retreat . . . nor ought any of this glory to be attributed to the Count de Lauzun or La Hougette, who at first left their men, but only to the valour and conduct of M. Zurlauben, Colonel of the Blue Regiment, who with unparalled bravery headed and brought off his men. [A]

Plunket states the 'heat of the action lasted not above one hour', and that the retreat was well-organised. [F] The French guns and Zurlauben's regiment kept the Williamites at bay. The River Nanny* was crossed successfully by the Jacobites and William's troops were too exhausted to follow up their victory. They had lost five hundred men to the Jacobites' one thousand. There is some argument for thinking that William was not keen to capture his father-in-law and anxious that he should be allowed to escape. In fact, James with a handful of men reached Dublin safely where he spent the night. Berwick sent him a message that horse and dragoons were needed to help cover the retreat, so three troops of Abercorn's horse and six troops of Luttrell's dragoons set off to join Berwick. Lauzun at Leixlip, a few miles west of Dublin, asked for all troops in Dublin to join him and said that James should make his way to France. James in retreat was always a sad figure. He was convinced that he was being hotly pursued and at a Mr Hacket's house, where he stopped, the meal he was given was scarcely touched. In Dublin he had met the Duchess of Tyrconnell, whom he told that the Irish had run well. 'You Sir seem to have beaten them,' she replied.

With the Duke of Powis, Henry Fitzjames and two troops of guards as

* Even today the Nanny, a small river, has only one narrow bridge across it at Duleek. The banks of the river are marshy and the bridge is covered by a hill on the south side that would, if fortified by artillery, prevent anyone else crossing.

escort, he set off for Bray, then Arklow, where he stopped at Mr Hacket's house, and here La Hougette and three other French officers caught up with him. The party went to Duncannon, where La Hougette found a French privateer that was prepared to take the king to Kinsale. There they found a French squadron under Foran and DuQuesne who took the King and the Marquis de Lery back to Brest. La Hougette and the other French officers made for Galway where they joined their regiments. The celebrated French general, the Marquis de Luxemburg, summed up the general feeling of the French court at seeing James return so quickly: 'Those who love the King of England must be very glad to see him safe and sound; but those who think of his reputation have reason to deplore the figure he has cut.' [H]

The battle had been a skirmish some said, just an organised retreat. Had James gone with his army to Limerick, this may have been the case. However, his decision, forced by his French advisors and by Tyrconnell, who knew what his queen desired, to flee to France made William the winner. The fact that Ireland still remembers the Boyne and forgets Aughrim is probably due to one king defeating another, rather than a Dutchman defeating a Frenchman. The question whether or not James should have fled so quickly from the scene is debatable. Tyrconnell was convinced that James could add nothing more to the war. There was still a Jacobite army in the field, but it needed reorganising. Nothing James could do at this moment would help, and if he was captured then the war would be over. The west of Ireland was still in Jacobite hands. The retreat went that way. Stevens reports that he got to Kilcullen on the road to Limerick when he

> . . . was overtaken by the Duke of Tyrconnell and his family, some whereof challenged the horse, and indeed he had the king's mark [Tyrconnell was using horses from James's stables]; they being too strong for us to cope with, for then might was the greatest right, they carried him away, leaving us afoot, weary and without friends or money.

The Boyne battle then was a decisive Williamite victory. The anniversary of the battle is still remembered, yet in Dublin it was only on 4 November that the Lords Justice held a Levée at the Castle, a procession and a banquet as this was William's birthday and the Dublin civil leaders did not want to celebrate a battle. In 1736 a commemorative obelisk was erected on the banks of the Boyne. It was destroyed in 1923 by the Irish army garrison in Drogheda because it had become the symbol of the Orange Order in Belfast. The statue to William in College Green, Dublin suffered as well and to find a statue today you have to go to St James's Square, London or to the small town of

A mural of the Battle of the Boyne on a cottage wall near Donore

Petersfield, Hampshire. In spite of the fact that the battle itself was a multi-national affair and men like Captain Stevens only fought to prevent being run down by his own cavalry in retreat, and then with arms he had purchased with money borrowed from a Protestant friend in Dublin, the battle is seen today as a triumph of Protestantism over Catholicism and banners of King Billy are carried in Orange Order marches. The truth is that one army beat the other because it was better led and organised. However, in spite of capturing Dublin the war was by no means over and much work was still to be done by William and his army.

Even when news of the Boyne reached England, Mary's first thoughts were of her husband, but she also must have had a sense of humour.

> Queen to King, 7 July: Expresses her joy at his victory at the Boyne. I must put you in mind of one thing, believing it now the season which is that you take care of the church in Ireland. Everybody agrees that it is the worst in Christendom. [E]

The departure of Marlborough and four thousand men from the Blackheath camp to Kinsale and Cork had left England very short of troops. True, there was a militia, but not much artillery. Nottingham wrote a memorandum to Mary suggesting that the small train of artillery in Portsmouth, that was not being used, should be returned to the Tower for 'further service'.

John Evelyn was kept busy visiting the Marquis de Ruvigny and his mother to console them on the death of the Marquis' brother, Caillemotte, at the Boyne (20 July), then on 1 August the Duke of Grafton who 'is going now to his ship at the mouth of the river (to transport him to Ireland, where he was slain).' [see pp. 58, 60]

On 12 August there was 'so great and long a storm of thunder & lightning as has seldom been seen in these countries.' On the thirteenth, Evelyn notes 'King James brought himself by a speedy flight and escape the sad tidings of his own defeat.' On the seventeenth, Evelyn gets news of:

> The sweet and hopeful youth, Sir Charles Tuke, died of the wounds he had received at the Boyne to the great sorrow of all his friends being I think the last male of that noble family . . . he was learned for his age, but was so unhappy to fall in that unhappy side of an unfortunate king.

Evelyn, like Pepys, moved in high society and London social life at the time was very much a question of routine parties, meeting people in church or in the park. He was related to the Tukes, a Roman Catholic family from Cressing Temple, Essex. Sir Charles was the son of Sir Samuel, one of Charles I's colonels, who Evelyn consulted about tree planting. Evelyn was very proud of his garden, which is mentioned by Pepys (Feb. 1669) and he was also a friend of the young Christopher Wren whom he met at the Royal Society. The two men got together to design a bee hive, modelled on the latest ideas practised by the Rev. Mew of Eastington, Gloucestershire, which when constructed was placed in a commanding position in the garden at Albury Park, Surrey.

Tuke was one of King James's life guards but his family were well known in court circles. On the nineteenth there was a day of thanksgiving for the success of King William and his escape (from a cannon ball) in Ireland.

The position of Catholics and Protestants in James II's reign needs a bit of explanation. The Archbishop of Canterbury, Sancroft, was an elderly man and did not object to James's open Catholic religion. However, Bishop Compton of London, the youngest son of a well-known Royalist Protestant family, was determined to put no encouragement in James's way. He was all for the Protestant succession. There was also the position of the dissenters, many of whom had supported Monmouth. They were disliked by the Anglicans and Catholics alike, but tolerated provided they didn't cause a nuisance. Pepys treated his Sunday visit to St Pauls or St Sepulcre's as a social excursion and commented on the sermon and on the pretty ladies present. He took one, Lady Paulina Montagu, to see the lions at the Tower of London and, later when she died, was very surprised that she had left a notebook recording the best sermons she had heard. He also has no kind word to say about William Penn, the Quaker. In December 1667, he records that:

> Mrs Turner (a friend who sits in the same pew at church) tells me that Mr William Penn, lately come over from Ireland, is a Quaker again or some very melancholy thing; that he cares for no company, nor comes into any; which is a pleasant thing, after his being abroad for so long and his father such a hypocritical rogue and at this time an atheist.

The country church was often in a similar state to that of today's church. People fell asleep and in Somerset one church appointed a bell ringer, paying him five shillings a year, to keep the congregation awake in the sermon. Quakers were reported for not attending but little was done about it. Travellers with licences to collect alms seldom went away unrewarded and bell ringers were paid to ring out for the queen's baby in 1688, and other historic events. Life went on as normal and men like Evelyn had friends in society who were both Catholic and Protestant.

5

The Naval Picture

William's navy that guarded his invasion fleet which took him to Torbay in 1688, was victorious thanks to the Protestant wind, and the good luck it had in avoiding Dartmouth's fleet, which might have stopped it reaching English shores. In fact, William instructed Admiral Herbert to avoid a sea battle and captains were instructed to shout out in English to their fellow sailors in Dartmouth's fleet not to fight for Popish tyranny against their old shipmates.

Thus the Dutch and English fleet became united and in theory should have had no problems putting the French fleet out of the Channel. However, the man William appointed as commander of his new fleet was not a Nelson. Thomas Herbert, who took over from Dartmouth in May 1689, attacked the French fleet that brought James II to Ireland in Bantry Bay. His eighteen ships of the line were outnumbered by the French, under the Marquis de Château-Renault who, however, was busy unloading equipment when Herbert's fleet appeared in the bay. The skirmish resulted in both fleets withdrawing, Herbert to the Scilly Isles and Château-Renault to Brest. The losses on both sides were small, no ships were sunk and Herbert was treated as a hero. William visited him when the fleet returned to Spithead, created him Earl of Torrington and knighted two of his captains, Ashby and Cloudsley Shovell. The sailors, who had no high opinion of their admiral, now called him 'Lord Tarry-town' as he liked the high life in court and was happy that his fleet remained in port.

In 1690 the French fleet got to sea before the English ships were ready. Their new admiral, the Comte de Tourville, was, it was said, capable of filling any post in his navy from carpenter to admiral. His signal notebook is still in existence and his sixty-eight ships constituted a much larger fleet than Torrington could put out, even with a Dutch contingent of twenty-two ships of the line, his twenty-one and Sir Ralph Delavall's thirteen, the allies were outnumbered. At Beachy Head, however, they did have the wind advantage and with the Dutch in the van bore down on the French who were in one long line, their admiral in the centre and out of position. Torrington in the centre steered for the French centre, but scarcely got close enough and in the battle the Dutch came off worst.

St James the Less, Teignmouth

The wind dropped at a crucial moment and damaged ships were towed away. The English fleet retreated into the mouth of the Thames using the ebb tide and the following day Tourville found he was master of the Channel. The French did not however make the most of their victory, men were falling ill, supplies were low and Tourville contented himself with an attack on the small, unimportant village of Teignmouth.

William's protracted absence in Ireland with the French fleet in the Channel caused some panic in England. John Evelyn, the diarist, who was an old man of seventy at the time, but kept in touch with court life, wrote on 6 July 1690:

> The whole nation now exceedingly alarmed by the French fleete braving our coast even to the very Thamesmouth [did he confuse the port of Teignmouth with Thames' mouth? It certainly seems like it unless this is a mistake of the Editor's]: our fleet commanded by debauched young men & likewise inferior in force, giving way to the enemy to our exceeding reproach.

The sacking of Teignmouth was not without incident. The town was deserted, the church which stands today about three hundred yards inland, looks like a castle, but then it was not so impregnable. The French landed in galleys, oar-driven by slaves, burnt the cottages, destroyed some fishing boats, destroyed the communion table and pulpit in the church and then hastily retired. The militia of Devon looked on in horror. They cheered, however, when two slaves escaped and swam for the shore. One drowned but the other, after an hour's swim, came safely ashore and was welcomed by the Devon people. Macaulay says that the man proved to be a Turk and was 'humanely sent back to his own people'. One hopes that this was what he wanted.

Meanwhile, Mary, who was in command with William away in Ireland, sent two of the Council, Lords Pembroke and Devonshire, to the fleet and they met up with Torrington at Deal, where he persuaded them that it was impossible now to carry on the action. They returned to Mary and reported. Arms were sent to the dockyards, the militia was called out, attacks were expected at both Portsmouth and Plymouth and the situation was very serious. Pepys, Clarendon and Dartmouth were sent to the Tower as suspected Papists – Dartmouth had commanded James's fleet and Clarendon was his father-in-law. All three were later released. The Dutch in particular were very displeased, demanding the repair of their ships and the dismissal of Torrington.

Pepys by this time was not a fit man. He was sixty-six, his wife had died in 1669 and he was trying to finish *Memoirs of the Navy*. In 1689 he was imprisoned for, it was thought, giving information to the French. Thus at this time he would be a suspect still, although living in Clapham with Mr Hewer, his former chief clerk, and a firm supporter of William and Mary's government.

The defences of England were not in great shape in early 1690 with most of the army being in Flanders and Ireland. Captain Thomas Phillips went to Portsmouth to try to improve its fortifications, earthworks were thrown up and pallisades, but two years later when the Duke of Leinster inspected the port, all seemed to have gone. The Isle of Wight defences were in an even poorer shape – Sandown Castle had vanished and only Carisbrook was in a defensible state. Hull and Berwick had some good Elizabethan defences but the former's were incomplete. Sir Martin Beckman reported to the House of Commons on the sad state of the defences, especially Portsmouth, but still nothing was done.

The five thousand foot and one thousand horse in England were supplemented by the militia, but the latter was local and did not move out of its own county. It was expensive to maintain – nearly forty thousand stood to at Plymouth – and by the end of August 1690 it was disbanded. Marines helped to man the Portsmouth defences and troops were brought back to London from Flanders and the crisis passed.

The 1692 scare was more serious. The army was by then back from Ireland, but so too were the Irish troops uncomfortably close in France. Nearly ten thousand troops were centred around Portsmouth under the command of Meinhard Schomberg, Bellasyse and Leinster. Brigadier Selwyn was put in command of London but the justices asked for Tollemache, the most popular of all English generals and they got him as soon as McKay could replace him in Flanders. Even at that stage William was more concerned to uphold his army in Flanders in priority to strengthening the English defences. Thus, as soon as the Battle of La Hogue (May 1692) was over, Tollemache was sent back to Flanders and only Leinster remained with his corps in Portsmouth with plans to make raids on the French coast.

Van Citters, one of William's Dutch advisers, wrote to Holland in August 1690 stating that:

> Throughout the country everyone on foot or horseback was under arms, which fact that all were embittered and motivated after the battle with the French, gave a tremendous peace of mind. The companies which I passed on the road did not sing anything else but 'God Bless William and Mary'.

The naval defeat of Beachy Head demanded a scapegoat. The Dutch in particular were furious that they had had to bear the brunt of the French fire. Pressure was put upon the government to court-martial Viscount Torrington. However Torrington defended his case very well. In spite of being sent to the Tower, at the court martial he was freed and the case against him thrown out. He stated in his defence:

> That our fighting upon so great a disadvantage as we did was of the last consequence to the kingdom, is as certain as that the Queen could not have been prevailed with to sign an order for it, had not both our weakness, and the strength of the enemy, been disguised to her.
>
> It is true, the French made not great advantage of their victory tho' they put as to a great charge in keeping up the militia; but had I fought otherwise, our fleet had been totally lost, and the kingdom had lain open to an invasion. What then would have become of us in the absence of His Majesty (in Ireland), and most of the land forces? As it was, most men were in fear that the French would invade, but I was always of another opinion; for I always said that whilst we had a *fleet in being*, they would not dare to make an attempt . . . whilst we observe the French, they can make no attempt either on sea or shore, but with great disadvantages; and if we are beaten all is exposed to their mercy. This I dare be bold to say, that if the management of the fleet had been left to the discretion of the council of war, there would have been no need of the excessive charge the kingdom was put to in keeping up the militia, nor would the French have gone off so much at their ease. [K]

In fact, the key words of Torrington, keeping 'A fleet in being' were the crux of the whole issue. The naval council realised the truth of this. Had Torrington not shut up the English fleet in the mouth of the Thames, the French could have defeated it and then run riot, perhaps even repeating De Ruyter and attacking the Medway.* Instead, he could spring back on the French whenever he wanted to and take them by surprise. The Royal Navy was not to forget this principle and it became one of supreme importance in the next one hundred and fifty years.

INTERLUDE AT CORK AND KINSALE

Ever since William had come to power in England, the Earl of Marlborough had felt neglected. He had been sent to support the Prince of Waldeck in Flanders with the Dutch and British army in their struggle against the French. In August 1689 thanks to a rather headstrong French commander, D'Humières, who led an attack on the hilltop town of Walcourt, Marlborough commanding the left wing and the Dutch infantry under Slangenburg on the right formed a pincer movement that nearly cut off the French. Only their cavalry prevented a rout. It was a much needed victory for the Anglo-Dutch forces.

Marlborough came home, however, to find the government in Mary's hands, William in Ireland and struggling against Limerick. What he needed was a show of force that would help his brother, a sailor – now a brigadier on land – to use four thousand troops and some marines to attack and capture Cork and Kinsale, the main ports used by the French for reinforcing the Jacobites. The council under Danby turned it down but Admiral Russell and Nottingham supported it and Mary wrote to her husband about it. He at once ignored his Dutch commanders and promised Marlborough cavalry support. William instructed him to take all munitions with him and use ships' guns.

The expedition set sail in eighty-two ships on 30 August 1690. One of the ships was commanded by the Duke of Grafton, who had fought with Marlborough at Sedgemoor. It was common at that time for soldiers to move from the army to the navy. Grafton, under suspicion as a Jacobite by birth, being the bastard son of Charles II and Barbara Villiers, was given command of a man-of-war, which he called the *Grafton.* Landing near Cork, Marlborough was joined by the Duke of Wurtemburg and

* In June 1667 De Ruyter's Dutch squadron entered the Thames and sailed up the Medway and captured the *Royal Charles* and burnt the other ships. 'God help us,' wrote Pepys, 'Home and to bed with a heavy heart.'

John Churchill, First Duke of Marlborough by Sir Godfrey Kneller

Sarah Churchill, Duchess of Marlborough After Sir Godfrey Kneller

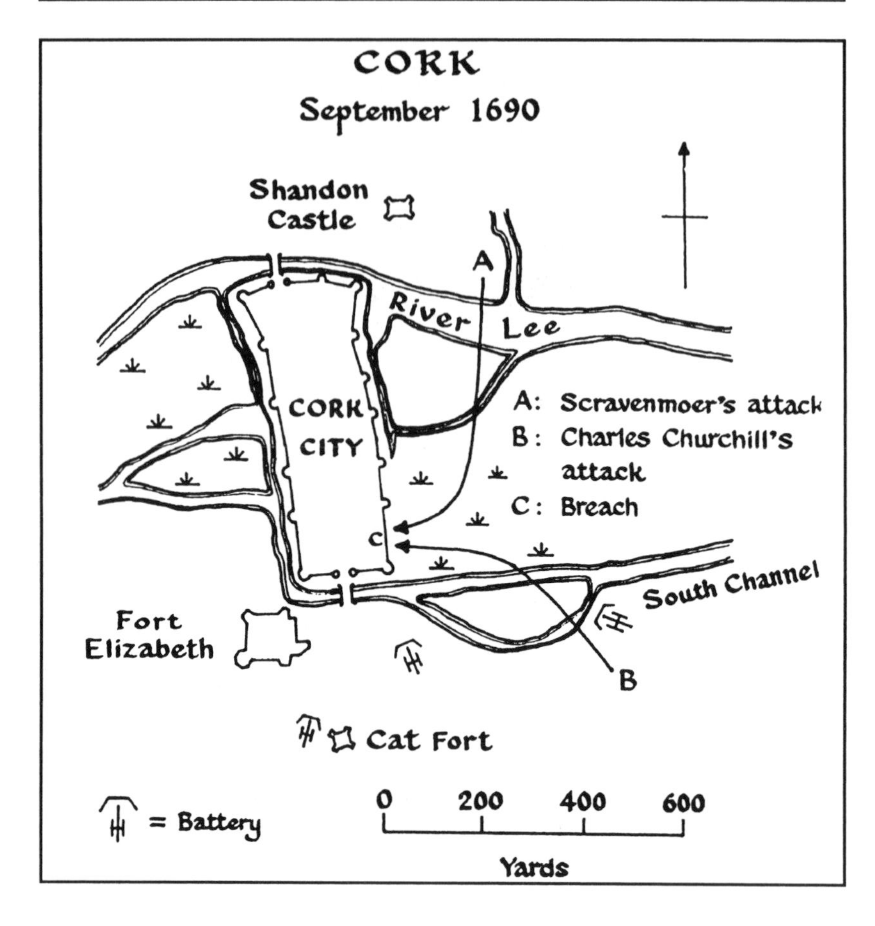

five thousand Danes, Dutch and Huguenot veterans of the Boyne. Grafton positioned the batteries and was mortally wounded whilst doing so. The Danes, Dutch and Huguenots under Scravenmoer, attacked over the River Lee and Brigadier Charles Churchill, Marlborough's brother, led the English across the South Channel into the breach made by Grafton's guns. The combined attack met with success.

The Duke of Berwick with a contingent of Jacobite cavalry looked on as the town was stormed. McElligott, the commander, surrendered and four thousand Jacobites were made prisoner. Marlborough contacted William about the prisoners and they were all put on a small island where many died of starvation. The episode was not forgotten in Cork, and although Marlborough sent £100 for their relief, it was, with Glencoe, an example of William's ruthlessness.

The stage was then set for Kinsale, some seventeen miles away. Situated on a bend in the Bandon River, it is well-protected by two forts; the Old Fort on the spit of land overlooking the town and the New Fort, now

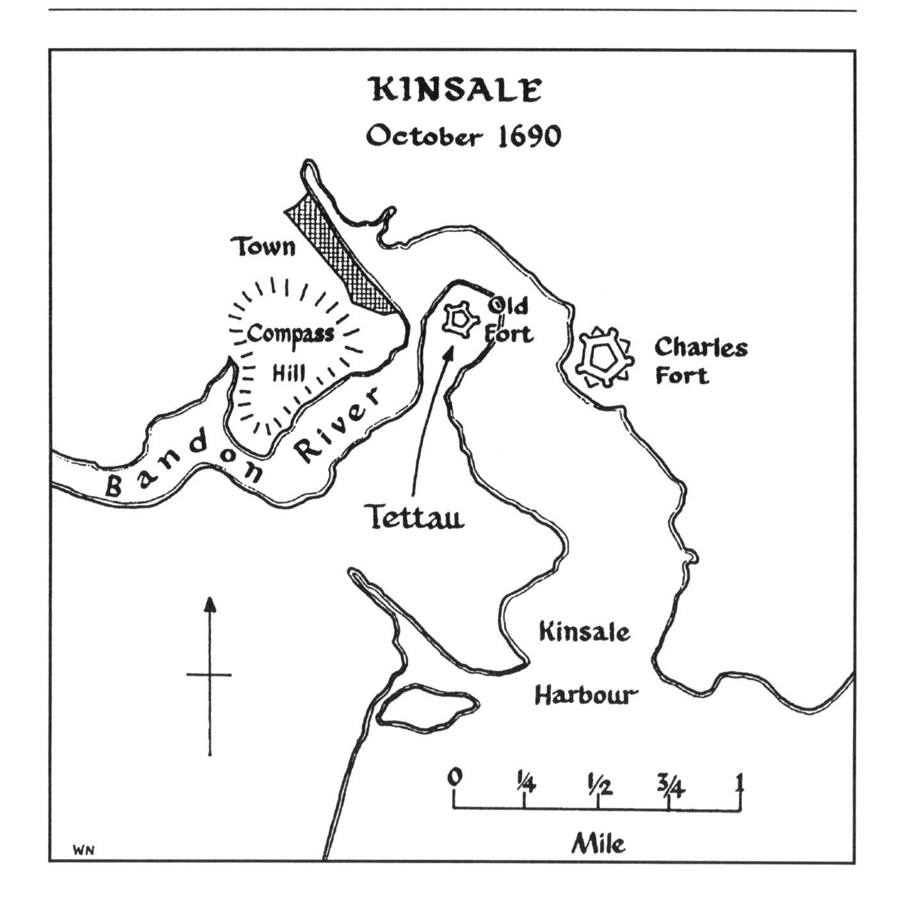

called Fort Charles, which is almost impregnable. The town is otherwise unprotected and Marlborough's cavalry soon seized it but they were unable to make any impression on the forts. The Danish second-in-command, Tettau, was given eight hundred men to storm the Old Fort. This he did in an early morning assault which, after some fierce fighting, succeeded.

Fort Charles was a different matter though. Its commander, Sir Edward Scott, refused to surrender. Saps were dug and the guns brought round from Cork. A breach was made with some difficulty as the trenches were filling with water. Marlborough approached Scott and summoned him to surrender. Fair terms were discussed and the garrison of twelve hundred men were allowed to march to Limerick, the men handing in their muskets but the officers keeping their swords. Brigadier Charles Churchill was made Governor of Kinsale, and Marlborough, well satisfied with the results of his campaign, in spite of losing Grafton and two hundred and fifty men, some to sickness, returned home to Portsmouth. 'No officer living', William wrote in French to his new commander, 'who has seen

Kinsale Harbour today

Charles Fort, Kinsale

so little service as My Lord Marlborough is so fit for great commands.' It was a two-edged compliment but any compliment at all from William was something.

William now came home himself, leaving Ginckel in charge of his army in Ireland, showing once again that he preferred his Dutch generals to his

English ones. However, General MacKay of Killicrankie fame, who had been fighting for William on the continent, now a major general, was sent to Ireland with General Tollemache, who had fought with Marlborough at Walcourt, and the Huguenot cavalry commander, the Marquis de Ruvigny. Over to the continent went Percy Kirke, who had relieved Londonderry but spent a long time doing it and Sir John Lanier and James Douglas who had helped Meinhard Schomberg at the Boyne. The stage was now set for a new offensive over the Shannon. William, perhaps realising at last how close he had been to death at the Boyne, was content to delegate authority. He knew Louis could only be contained on the continent and he was anxious to discover how Mary was coping without him. England and his wife wanted him home.

One of the immediate results of Marlborough's successful capture of Cork and Kinsale was that supplies could now be sent there from England's West Country ports. There is a record of the Irish Committee in London, which consisted of Marlborough, Nottingham, Sydney, Sir Henry Goodricke (Chief of Ordnance) and William Blathwayte sending the following arms to Ireland on 7 April 1691: [P]

To Kinsale by the:

	Pikes	*Snaphaunces*	*Matchlocks*	*Carbines*	*Pistols*
Charles	–	640	850	510	270
St Thomas	2000	1900	–	–	470
Henry and William	1036	1100	–	–	460
Brethren of Hastings	–	–	–	–	–

To Dublin by the:

	Pikes	*Snaphaunces*	*Matchlocks*	*Carbines*	*Pistols*
Biscay Merchant	–	–	–	525	480 prs
Susannah	–	–	–	40	320 ps
Speedwell	–	–	500	505	–
Barnstaple Market	1000	–	–	–	–
Endeavour	–	–	–	–	–

Total:		
	Snaphaunces:	3640
	Matchlocks:	1350
		4990

The snaphaunce was an early type of flintlock, the carbines were for dragoons, the pikes for infantry and the matchlocks for dragoons or infantry. The pairs of pistols were for officers or cavalrymen and the *Brethren of Hastings* and *Endeavour* may well have had troops on board as well as being armed sloops. The *Speedwell*, a new ship, was built in 1690 and was a fifth-rater which meant she carried approximately thirty-six cannon and nearly two hundred men. It is surprising that the ship from Barnstaple was heading for Dublin not Kinsale, but at least the supplies no longer had to take the overland route to Chester then be carted down south from Carrickfergus or Belfast.

In 1692 the French were at last ready to invade England. An army of twenty thousand was assembled at the ports of Cherbourg, Le Havre and La Hogue in Normandy. The Irish troops, ferried over in November and December 1691 from Limerick and Cork in English ships, were part of the force. King James came to La Hogue to see them. It must have been a magnificent spectacle and William must have had second thoughts about his rash plan to permit the French army to take in all the Irish Jacobites. Tourville was again in command and it was hoped that he would be joined by the Toulon fleet, but the latter was so disturbed by bad weather that it did not arrive in Brest until July. The English Jacobites were boasting that the British fleet captains would desert to the Jacobites once they realised that King James, their old commander, was present.

Nevertheless even without the Toulon fleet, Tourville set sail from Brest with forty-five ships of the line and seven fireships to try and stop the Dutch and British fleets from uniting. Russell, who had replaced Torrington, joined up with the Dutch at Rye and having sent two scouting fleets ahead under Carter and Delaval, he waited for them to return off the Isle of Wight. The combined Anglo-Dutch fleet thus consisted of ninety-nine ships of the line with no less than thirty-seven frigates and fireships. The three squadrons were commanded by Russell, Delaval and Shovell (Red); Ashby, Rooke and Carter (Blue) and Allemonde's Dutch squadron (White). The weather was foggy and Russell, with the wind in his favour, sailed for Cape Harfleur. There was a plan to land troops at St Malo, but it seems neither side knew exactly where the other was so it must have been a shock for Tourville when the fog lifted and he saw the size of his enemy. The Battle of La Hogue lasted for three days. Rooke, in front of King James and others on shore, entered the bay of La Hogue and burnt or destroyed every French ship he could find. Delaval did the same at Cherbourg, Tourville and a few others escaped by taking the dangerous passage between Alderney and Cherbourg. Some French ships shut themselves in St Malo and later escaped to Brest, others went all around the British Isles as had the Armada, before returning to Brest. It was a complete victory. For James the invasion was off, the French fleet was shut out of the Channel and the Irish troops were left to join the army of Marshal Luxembourg. It was an unexpected twist to the victory. Had the invasion taken place, the Irish might have been defeated at sea or on the shores of Sussex, as it was they marched off to do battle with William's forces in the land war.

We must look, though, at what the French navy had achieved in the last two years in its supply convoys to Ireland. D'Anfreville's fleet of thirty-six ships took Lauzun and his six thousand French troops to Kinsale in March 1690 and brought back to France the Mountcashel brigade. Supplies that came in at Tyrconnell's request included brass (for coin-making), tents, shirts, ammunition, carts, harness, tools, flour, wine and brandy. The fleets were organised by the Minister of Marine, Seignelai, who usually had to argue the case with Louvois before sending anything, or especially anyone, to Ireland. However, there was a small grain fleet under Forant that went to Kinsale in June which by coincidence arrived to take away King James after the Boyne. Forant also took supplies to Limerick – mostly flour, grain, wine and brandy.

In August 1690, Admiral D'Anfreville was back with a fleet to take the French troops out of Galway. There was an argument with Lauzun over horses; he and other French officers wanted to take their Irish horses with them but D'Anfreville refused, saying the boats were unsuitable. This trip to France was also made by Tyrconnell who earned the gratitude of the French sailors by giving them a pound of fresh meat a day. D'Anfreville was critical of the biscuit left behind for the Irish soldiers. 'One would not give to Algerians returning to Barbary, biscuit such as that' he reports to Seignelai, giving the blame to Forant. [L]

Seignelai died in November and the new fleet controller was the former financial controller, Pontchartrain, who was only keen to use the navy if it was back again in small fleet with *Chef d'Escadre* Nesmond in command. M. des Anges brought the rest of the fleet to Galway with a combined cargo of rope, arms, tools, back-baskets (used for carrying stones in sieges as well as supplies), sacks, shirts, powder and ammunition. The three French engineers Robert, La Combe and Methelet also arrived. The English fleet made no move to stop these valuable supplies from reaching Limerick. It had no port on the west coast of Ireland and was too busy escorting army supplies to Carrickfergus and, after the capture of Cork and Kinsale, to these two ports as well. On 19 May, twenty-five ships arrived with the new French general, St Ruth and his deputies D'Usson, de Tessé and La Tour Monfort. This fleet had coats for all Irish soldiers, ammunition, flour, iron, steel and rope, saddles, harness, tents and sixteen French artisans, presumably for working on siege lines, repairing guns etc.

The sixth and largest French fleet sailed in October. It arrived at

Limerick too late, for the town had surrendered to William three weeks earlier. One does not know what happened to the arms. ammunition, tents and harness etc. Presumably the provisions were all eaten, but the ships returned to Brest with part of the Irish army and their servants, women and children. Louvois had died and it was Louis himself who arranged this fleet. Would it have saved the day had it come earlier? It is unlikely, as Sarsfield and the Irish leaders had already decided to surrender on conditions. The Irish leader was keen to go to France where he could carry on the struggle. He had seen the devastation it had caused in his country and he knew that an invasion of England was possible from France. Strangely enough Ginckel was happy to help. In fact the French fleet arrived to help Ginckel decide on getting the troops away. So it may have prevented more lives from being lost.

To sum up, La Hogue was a great victory and completely put James's plans for an invasion out of the picture. Only the few French ships who reached St Malo escaped destruction. Tourville's luck had run out. Yet he was, like Torrington, only obeying orders. Both had made the best of a bad run of luck and Torrington had saved the Anglo-Dutch fleet. Henceforward William's navy could bombard French ports at will, which they proceeded to do. Only the French privateers under commanders like Jean Bart, kept the British navy on their toes. It wasn't for another fifty years in 1745 that the French combined again with the Jacobites for a plan to attack Britain.

Why hadn't either William or Louis attempted to keep supplies from entering Ireland? Louvois and Louis himself were anxious to keep William in Ireland with his army as long as possible, hence the sixth fleet arriving after Limerick with yet more supplies. This was their policy. William's army had a short route to get to Ireland and it was difficult for the French to stop. The Battle of Bantry Bay was the only attempt made by William's fleet to keep out the French. They could have made more effort but their ships were needed elsewhere: as convoy support, taking troops to Holland, guarding the shores of England. The Irish waters are not easy to defend and until Marlborough captured Cork and Kinsale in 1690 and William captured Waterford, everything centred on Carrickfergus which, though it had a castle to defend it, was too far to the north. Dublin Bay never became a major port in the war. Rooke attacked it once when the French were there, with some success, at least enough to stop them using it again. However, the British navy liked to be near a home port – Portsmouth or Plymouth – and the Irish ports were not equipped for repairs, stores and taking on fresh hands. The age of the blockade was still to come.

6

The First Siege of Limerick

The Irish cavalry officer, Patrick Sarsfield, now came into his own. His portrait shows him to be tall, good looking in a very Stuart way with thick lips and curly long hair. He was born in 1655, so was younger than Marlborough and James. He joined the French army as a young man and seemed to have been involved in various scrapes and duels. In 1685 he joined Colonel Oglethorpe's troop of horse and at Sedgemoor he was surrounded by club-carrying rebels, knocked off his horse and left for dead. He soon recovered and was made a captain in Richard Hamilton's regiment of dragoons. His military career really started here and, although at the Boyne he had only been in charge of James's personal escort, after it he then became the Irish army leader.

Tyrconnell had retreated into his shell; perhaps, as a man of sixty, he realised his time was up as far as rallying a defeated army went. Lauzun and the French officers, with one exception, went to Galway and prepared to escape back to France so Sarsfield now exerted his influence. James had left his son, the twenty-year-old Duke of Berwick in command, and he presided at the first Council of War in Limerick. Limerick was defended by the French officer De Boisseleau, who had elected to stay while his fellow French officers deserted. Sarsfield, who was some fifteen years older than Berwick, considered the latter's plan to take the three and a half thousand-strong Irish cavalry on a raid of Dublin rash and stupid. Sarsfield, whom King James had called a blockhead, came up with an ingenious plan that if it came off would end the war at a stroke. The artillery attack on King William before the Boyne had come within a hair's breadth of success. Why not kidnap him? The king was often seen with an escort of no more than a few men, ADCs and messengers mostly – unlike King James who usually moved with two troops of Lifeguards, this king was more of a loner. The opportunity came when William's army finally arrived at Limerick.

A cavalry squadron spotted King William, attended by Count Schomberg and a few others, on a slight hill watching the walls of the city to see where the best place to attack might be. The cavalry crossed a ford to attempt to cut off the king. Luckily they were spotted in time by Schomberg's equerry who warned the king. The king laughed at him,

Richard Talbot, Earl of Tyrconnell, James II's Lord Deputy of Ireland by François de Troy

Patrick Sarsfield
Attributed to John Riley

but the equerry suddenly swore and helped the surprised king into his saddle. They were just in time and Count Schomberg's horse was killed in the swift escape. [G]

Sarsfield now had a second and better idea. A Huguenot artillery man had deserted to the Jacobites and told them that a siege train was on its way from Dublin several miles behind the main army. The details of the train are known to us (see Chapter 2). There were two hundred and eight men, mostly civilian waggoners, but also wheelwrights, smyths, Gentlemen of the Ordnance, tynmen to look after the pontoons, and twenty-four gunners with a small escort of fusiliers. There were no less than nine thousand, nine hundred horses and hay for same with £56.5s worth of looping or bridles for these horses. [D] A Dutch engineer, William Meesters, was nominally in command, but Colonel Villiers' regiment of cavalry was present as escort and no doubt Captain Poulteney, their commander, decided on how much ground they covered each day and consulted the Dutchman on matters to do with guns. A print [G] shows three horses per cannon. Each cannon was looped up to the three horses and a man guided them over the roads. The end of the towing arm fitted over a spike and two extra wheels so that in effect the cannon with four wheels could move quicker, at least on good roads, than if it had only two wheels. Heavy cannon were prone to get stuck in the mud and sometimes as many as ten horses would be required to be looped up to pull the guns out of a bog or river bed. The train moved very slowly.

Sarsfield planned an attack on the train. He obtained permission for this from Tyrconnell, still nominally commander-in-chief of the army, and from Major-General Sheldon who commanded the cavalry. The defended post at Annaghberg on the Shannon was abandoned, the gunners moving to Limerick and the horse joining Sarsfield. He collected six hundred men, the best riders he could find. Sarsfield led them to Killaloe, twelve miles up stream from Limerick. Scouts were sent out to find out where the train was. In the Silvermine Mountains, Sarsfield's horsemen were well hidden.

Ginckel, however, with Kirke and some cavalry, noticed early next morning that the Annaghberg ford was undefended. They waded over and were surprised that the Irish trenches were unmanned and there were signs of a hurried departure. Why they didn't guess that some five hundred Jacobite horse had crossed the Shannon is a mystery.

On 11 August, a Mr O'Brien, a local farmer from the Silvermine Mountains, came into William's camp with news that horses had crossed the Shannon at Killaloe in the night. No one believed him [G] but a sergeant and a few horse went off to Killaloe to check O'Brien's story. The sergeant came back with plenty of evidence from local people who had heard the horsemen go by. William left affairs to the Earl of Portland, who left them to Sir John Lanier, who was slow to do anything about it.

The two-mile train was near to Tipperary by the ruins of Ballyneety castle, where it spent the night. A party of horse under Cunningham was spotted consulting with Poulteney, but it moved off. Sarsfield, now in a concealed position overlooking Ballyneety, realised he must work fast or the train's escort would be reinforced. Sending young Captain Fitzgerald and a troop of horse to ambush Cunningham if he returned, Sarsfield went on the attack. Guided by local rapparees under their leader Hogan, the Irish horsemen approached the English camp. It was a moonlit night and the waggons and guns stood out clearly for Sarsfield, but it was not too bright for sentries to recognise him as an enemy.

There is a conical rock near the church at Templebredan which is supposed to be where the artillery train camped and the waggoners lit their fires. The cavalry camped a few yards away, their horses not easily to hand. The password was, unfortunately for the train defenders, 'Sarsfield' and the leader is supposed to have shouted out 'Sarsfield is the word and Sarsfield is the man'. The horsemen charged down at the unsuspecting convoy at midnight. There was chaos: Poulteney scarcely got his boots on, men were cut down in a cornfield, Meesters dived into a bed of nettles and others hid in a wood. Some women were killed in the mêlée, but it was Sarsfield who soon restored order: 'Burn and destroy everything' he said. Waggons were overturned and the horses were rounded up. The guns were a problem but a captured artilleryman helped with advice, he suggested that to destroy a cannon you load it with powder and dig a pit in which you put the barrel. This took time and only two or three of the cannon were actually destroyed, the rest falling out of their holes with the explosion. The pontoons were easier to hole with picks and bayonets. The powder barrels were emptied – no one thought of carrying them to Limerick where they could have been useful, similarly the food stores. A waggon loaded with money for the army remained unseen and undisturbed. It was the only piece of luck William was to have that night.

In Limerick, Lanier's force had set off to meet the train. When they heard the explosions they knew O'Brien had been right and, changing direction, set off for the ford at Killaloe. Here they waited in vain all night as Sarsfield, like the three wise men, had an inkling that all would be on watch for him, so he returned to Limerick by a different and longer route. Only Captain Fitzgerald and his men had bad luck that night when Cunningham found them and killed fifteen of them including their luckless leader.

Rowland Davies left an account of the scene of the attack on the train.

An army chaplain from Cork, he was not prone to make up stories. 'We found many men killed. I believe about fifty and of them most were in the train', he wrote, but he made no mention of women and children being murdered. In Dublin Dean Harrison was one of those responsible for the rumour that woman and children camp followers had been killed and thrown on the fires, but the rumour went unsupported and those who knew Sarsfield did not believe it.

At a stroke, William had lost two guns which had been totally destroyed and four others which were unusable. The horses had been taken away, the cannonballs lost or scattered, the powder burned, the food destroyed, waggons overturned, pontoons holed and, when Cunningham reached Ballyneety, the money waggon and the remaining six cannons were all that was left to guard. [G]

The effect on morale in the Irish camp was tremendous. The Irish troops toasted Sarsfield, and De Boisseleau had more volunteers than he needed to strengthen the Limerick defences. We must now look at the first siege of Limerick and see what took place. De Boisseleau and his men had not been idle and the city was now well-prepared for a siege.

William realised that the Boyne had only been the beginning. The Jacobite headquarters was next on the list. If he captured this the war would be over. Sarsfield, however, had anticipated this and, remembering the ineffective siege guns of Londonderry, had acted quickly to remove William's train.

It is true that William had lost his siege train but he still had some 12 pdr. guns and some heavier guns were brought from Waterford, now in his hands. After a week he captured the Star Fort and he ordered Wurtemburg, Tettau and Kirke to attack the advanced redoubt. Initially repulsed, some guns were brought up and the garrison suffered. De Boisseleau, however, brought up Colonel Fitzgerald (no relation to Captain Fitzgerald) and a hundred and fifty marksmen in the night and positioned Lord Kilmallock's cavalry to fall on the attacking group the following morning. This was successful and the Danes and Prussians were beaten back. More fighting ensued before the redoubt was eventually captured by the Williamites. William now placed five 24 pdr. guns in the redoubt along with his 36 pdr. gun. Then he battered down a large breach in the walls. It took five days of bombardment to make a hundred-yard breach. Inside, however, De Boisseleau ordered a second inner wall to be built with a firing step. Here the Grand Prior's regiment took their positions as Captain Stevens of the Grand Prior regiment tells us. Three small cannon were placed to fire into the breach. On the afternoon of 6 September, the attack came.

Led by the Brandenburghers, the infantry stormed in and the cannon

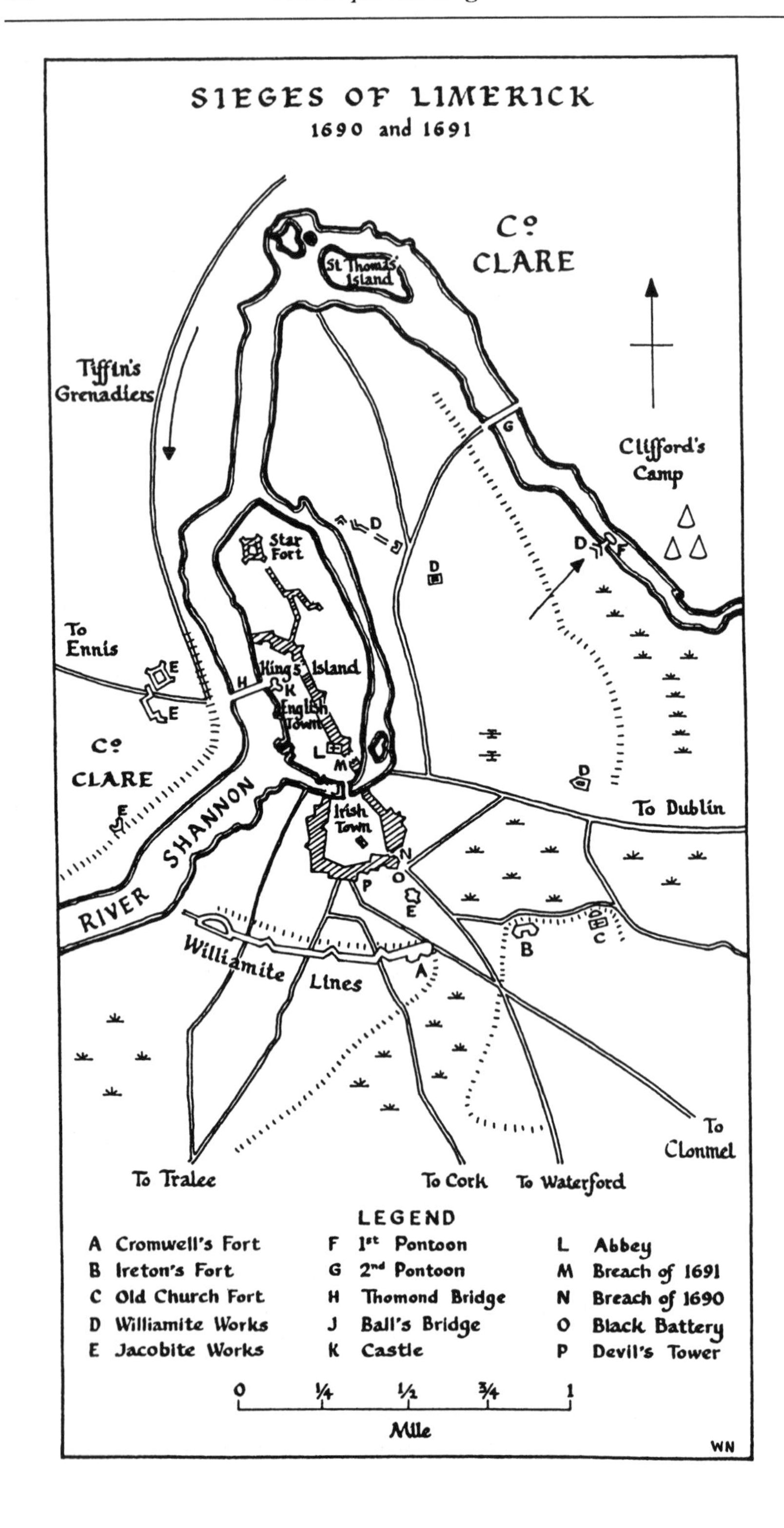
SIEGES OF LIMERICK
1690 and 1691
Co CLARE
St Thomas's Island
Tiffin's Grenadiers
Clifford's Camp
Star Fort
To Ennis
King's Island
English Town
Co CLARE
RIVER SHANNON
Irish Town
To Dublin
Williamite Lines
To Tralee
To Cork
To Waterford
To Clonmel
LEGEND
A Cromwell's Fort
B Ireton's Fort
C Old Church Fort
D Williamite Works
E Jacobite Works
F 1st Pontoon
G 2nd Pontoon
H Thomond Bridge
J Ball's Bridge
K Castle
L Abbey
M Breach of 1691
N Breach of 1690
O Black Battery
P Devil's Tower
0 ¼ ½ ¾ 1
Mile
WN

opened up on them. Stevens' men opened fire and so too did De Boisseleau's regiment. Their captain dropped but his place was taken by another officer. The Macmahon regiment on the ramparts threw stones. For almost two hours the assault went on until the grenadiers staggered back, many wounded, most of them covered in dust and blood. It was a severe setback. Meanwhile, two English regiments had been launched at the St John's Gate. They did not get far before the fire of Maxwell's and Talbot's dragoons drove them off in great disorder. The Black Battery was causing a problem by firing across the attackers. This was so named as it was on the flank and built of stone that had turned black with age and presumably smoke. It was also manned by some determined defenders. William gave orders for his Brandenburghers to charge it. This they did, but a tremendous explosion threw both attackers and defenders into the air. There were few survivors.

That night in Cromwell's Fort, William was depressed. Things had not gone well, the weather was now against the besiegers and trenches were filling with rain water. His Brandenburghers looked like 'Furies with the misfortune of gunpowder'. Some three thousand men had already been lost, more than all the Boyne casualties put together while the Irish had lost four hundred men at the most. In De Cambon's Huguenot regiment only six officers were fit to serve, and the other Huguenot regiments suffered badly, as did those of Douglas, (which had already been repulsed at Athlone,) Cutts, Stuart and Meath. The Danes had forty-five junior officers killed or disabled.

The Rev. Story, the army chaplain in William's camp, has left a graphic description of the horror of this day.

> From half an hour after three until seven there was one continued fire of both great and small shot without any intermission: insomuch that the smoke reached in one continuous cloud to the top of the mountain at least six miles off.

A drummer boy was sent to De Boisseleau to request permission to bury the dead. It was refused and they remained on the shattered walls of Limerick. The civilians killed would have been buried after the action in the churchyard, but a great number had left the town before the siege. De Boisseleau would have seen to this so that there would be empty houses for his troops and enough food to go round.

De Boisseleau reported back to France that:

> Officers in the defending force greatly distinguished themselves during a siege of 21 days of open trenches, and the Irish soldiers not merely fought

> well but sustained with extraordinary patience all the fatigues which were very great, seeing that they were always under arms, and that they were in want of the simplest necessities of life. Brigadier John Hamilton assisted me with constancy and ability.

It was a disaster for the Williamites. One of the reasons for abandoning the siege after barely three weeks can be culled from the pages of *Tristram Shandy* by Lawrence Sterne. Corporal Trim states that those who could afford it burnt bowls of spirit in their tents to keep out the damp. The besiegers in Ireland seemed to suffer more than the besieged – at least the latter could live in houses or cellars and were not prone to the terrible weather conditions. The unhappy William left for England. He appointed the Dutchman, Count Solms, to command his army and three Lord Justices to govern the country.

The victories of Fleurus, Beachy Head and Staffarda (on 18 August when Catinat's French army overwhelmed the Duke Victor of Savoy) must have been a blessing to King Louis. He would not have been amused at having James back so suddenly with news of his own defeat. Generals who fled from the scene of action were not popular (as General Cope found out in 1745), so in spite of the safe return of Lauzun and most of the French troops from Galway, Louis was not keen to send another French army to help in Ireland. It was Tyrconnell who went over to put his position to the French court, who was successful in obtaining a new general, arms and powder, but he failed to get French troops. The French navy were running out of ports and also Louis was running out of enthusiasm for supporting James. His one aim had been to tie down William in Ireland for as long as possible so that he had the option of descending on England or on the Netherlands, where the Allies were weak.

The Boyne had caused Louis to think again. He sent St Ruth, the hammer of the Huguenots, to Ireland as a suitable leader, or was it to get rid of one of his more troublesome generals? There is no doubt he must have been aware that neither Schomberg nor Ruvigny would have been available to help William had it not been for the policy of driving out the Huguenots from France. The French who fought at the Boyne were on both sides, the Huguenots on William's side were victorious, the defeated French Catholics came home. Marlborough was aware that his army which was withdrawn from Flanders to England at the time of the Boyne, was not strong enough to defend England; but it was strong enough to attack Cork and Kinsale, and put out two ports that were supplying

James's army from France. This was evident too to William. He disliked English generals, but he was clever enough to see when they had a good plan. He laid the ground for Marlborough's later career and would have deservedly taken some of the credit for the duke's famous victories in the years ahead.

Meanwhile, Tyrconnell, who had avoided the horrors of Limerick as he had been at Galway, decided to go to France and report on the situation in Ireland to James, his king. He sailed in September with Lauzun and De Boisseleau and the French troops that had played so little part at the Boyne. Berwick was left as Vice-Viceroy as Tyrconnell had too much at stake not to return. A small force under Berwick himself attempted to capture Birr Castle but Kirke was in the vicinity at Roscrea and Berwick retired. Berwick's time as commander-in-chief was drawing to an end, for a further delegation was sent to France to put James and Tyrconnell in the picture and also to plead for more French reinforcements and money.

In the Williamite army, Count Solms was soon replaced by Ginckel. The latter was instrumental in suppressing a mutiny in 1688 when the Royal Scots, or some of them, refused to go to the continent to fight under a Dutch officer. The mutineers made their way home from Ipswich. Ginckel and his cavalry overtook them in Lincoln and, with the loss of only one life, persuaded them to return south, making sure they were paid to do so. Ginckel had fought bravely at the Boyne and was popular with the troops regardless of their nationality and was determined to do better than old Schomberg's policy of doing nothing in the winter. Dividing his army into four groups, Ginckel and Scravenmoer moved against Limerick for a second attempt. The city was now governed by General Dorrington. Von Tettau moved into County Kerry. General Douglas moved against Sligo and Kirke and Lanier were instructed to force a passage over the Shannon. These three were replaced before the Aughrim campaign had started.

The Danes were unsuccessful in Kerry. Ross Castle near Killarney held out and they had insufficient artillery to level it. In January, Wurtemberg marched on Kilbolane Castle in County Cork. The garrison withdrew, setting fire to it first. There was continual trouble from 'rapparees', the Irish equivalent of the clubmen in England during the Civil War. These malcontents banded together and stole horses which they sold, ambushed supply wagons and generally played one side against another.

The discipline in the Danish contingent was strict. One of the rittmeisters (captains) was cashiered after a report from his commanding officer, Major-General von Tettau, reached the Duke of Wurtemberg. The report concerned a cavalry action in which the rittmeister took to his heels. There is a graphic description of the Danes in this action in a document from the Copenhagen archives. Von Tettau was given the following report by the officer commanding the Danish post at Fermoy Bridge:

> Yesterday at 10 p.m. Rittmeister Schliebe went from here with a forage party to take sheep from the enemy. At 3.00 p.m. today the party came back in a state as I have never seen. The trumpeter rode in front blowing the alarm. Here came five troopers, there six, here ten, all scattered. And at the bridge [of Fermoy] there was such confusion as they [the guard] would not let them cross that they went through the water here and there. They did not know what strength the enemy followed them for they were not yet engaged with them. The number of the enemy whom I saw might have been 40 or 50 who followed the wretched troopers to within a cannon shot of the bridge. I had to look on while a corporal and 4 men were attacked by the enemy in this confusion not more than a 1000 paces from the bridge. All had flintlocks and defended themselves bravely, but the troopers acted very badly and deserted them completely. I ordered a lieutenant and 50 musketeers to go to their assistance. They rescued two, but the corporal was taken prisoner and one of the four shot dead. The Rittmeister cuts a sorry figure and complains he was unable to keep his men in order. He had taken a lieutenant prisoner in his quarters close to Bellinahinsche, but when pursued by the enemy he let him escape. The lieutenant came himself to the bridge and . . . he wishes to join King William's service. His name is Jan Wizchert of Col.Lessi's Regiment. I have kept him here awaiting the Major General's orders. Would he agree to write to the [Jacobite] commander at Bellinahinsche on the possibility of getting the corporal back. The lieutenant says that his captain was in charge of the party and assures me we will get the corporal back as his captain is quite a reasonable man. He tells me that his garrison had news yesterday from Limerick that 6,000 cavalry and dragoons, as well as ammunition and six months' pay had arrived in Galway from France. [This was wishful thinking.] Also that his garrison were in daily expectation that Sarsfield would arrive with a force including artillery. The carpenter is strengthening the bridge; this will be completed within 5 days. If such a force comes to attempt our line Fermoy bridge will be the first they will try and attack. I await orders what to do with the lieutenant and also three other prisoners, and so remain my noble Major General's most obliged and obedient servant, Boyneburg. [L]

Meanwhile, Tyrconnell had not been idle in France. He knew what was required – a competent leader – and he had found one. The Marquis of St Ruth had been Louis' commander in Savoy – he is called St Rhue by one authority – but to all and sundry he is known as St Ruth. Proud and vain according to Berwick, he was a shrewd tactician and he was accompanied by his deputies De Tessé and D'Usson. None of them seemed to have much English and communications were to be a problem. He brought some artillery officers, cloth for twenty thousand uniforms, arms, food but no money to speak of. Henceforward the Irish Jacobite army was to prove more of a fighting force than it had been before. Ginckel was in for something of a shock.

7

The Siege of Athlone

After the successful defence of Limerick, the Jacobite leaders quarrelled amongst themselves. It was the first time they had had the opportunity to do so since before the Boyne, and some looked round to see who to blame for that disaster.

The scapegoat of the Boyne was at first Tyrconnell, who seemed to have gone into a decline and was reluctant to do anything. Sarsfield wanted to dispose of him and went to the Duke of Berwick, who was nominally in command after his father's exile. Berwick did not want to get involved and said that Tyrconnell was still Viceroy and there was still a campaign to be fought. The matter died down though it did nothing to improve morale in the Irish army.

The French, meanwhile, who had few casualties at the Boyne and had not thrown away their arms, moved to Galway where they prepared to embark for France. They, as Macaulay has said, were sick of Ireland:

> The climate affected their health and spirits. In that unhappy country, wasted by years of predatory war, hospitality could offer little more than a couch of straw, a trencher of meat half raw and half burned, and a draught of sour milk. A crust of bread, a pint of wine, could hardly be purchased for money . . . better to be a prisoner in the Bastille, better to be a recluse in La Trappe, than to be generalissimo of the half naked savages who burrowed in the dreary swamps of Munster.

Tyrconnell joined Lauzun in Galway and left Limerick to the Marquis De Boisseleau, who promptly ordered his deputy, Brigadier Wauchope, to improve the town's defences. The breastworks and ditches constructed outside the city walls would do much to keep out William's tired soldiers.

Meanwhile at Athlone, the town bridge across the Shannon had been broken and Colonel Grace, a Civil War veteran, was in command in the castle with a small garrison. William, engaged in Waterford, sent Major-General Douglas with a small force to capture Athlone, and Sarsfield with a larger force of cavalry and guns went from Limerick to reinforce Grace. After a week, Douglas, whose guns were not powerful

Athlone Castle today

enough to make any impression on Athlone Castle, retired to Mullingar telling William that his artillery needed strengthening.

Douglas wrote a letter, which has survived, to William:

> I have done my best endeavours at Athlone. The necessaries which belong to our train were so small that even powder was scarce. At the beginning we had but 18 barrels of powder for 10 pieces of cannon and 2 howitzers. They make head at Rachray which is fourteen miles distant from my camp. All their passes on the Shannon and many more the enemy had possessed before I came here, or at least the next day after, so that it is generally believed that they will endeavour to keep the Prince of Connaught [Athlone or does he mean Limerick?] for their winter quarters, and hereby prolong the war, or obtain terms for themselves – this reason is likewise my not having powder to make a breach on their retrenchment. Its made me judge it absolutely necessary at present to retire to Mullingar. [E]

Douglas then joined William at Catherconlish and took part in the first siege of Limerick. He was then sent home.

The second siege of Athlone started in June 1691. Ginckel's army of about twenty thousand was accompanied by no less than thirty-two guns, six mortars and one thousand cannonballs for each piece. There was an Irish garrison at Ballymore, only five hundred men under Colonel Ulrick Burke, but he held out to the first field guns that opened up on his defences. The main guns came up and for four hours the soldiers had a grandstand view of their artillery in action. Story relates that:

> All our guns and mortars fell to work . . . the bombs tearing up the sandy banks, and the Irish running like conies from one hole to another; whilst the guns were battering the works and making a breach, the Irish in the meantime did what they could with their two guns and small shot; but Lieutenant.Col.Burton, their engineer had his hand shot off from one of our batteries, and their works went down apace which made the Irish very uneasy.

Burke hoisted a white flag, the cannonade continued a while, then Ginckel, accepting Burke's plea of surrender at last, sent the Irish to Dublin as prisoners. He waited at Ballymore for his pontoons then proceeded slowly to Athlone.

St Ruth had plenty of time to see the defences. Grace had simply abandoned the eastern town, withdrawing over the bridge to the better defended western town with its castle. He had burnt most of the eastern town, which was abandoned, and broken the bridge. Sarsfield had helped build up the earthworks and ditches protecting the bridge at both ends. On 19 June, Ginckel was in a position to start the siege and the following day his guns opened up. Wauchope, commanding the musketeers on the Leinster side was crushed by masonry and carried over the bridge to safety. The Grand Prior regiment took their turn in the defences and Stevens complained of falling rocks being more dangerous than shells or cannon balls. He was glad when his men were replaced. St Ruth had worked out a rota for regiments to relieve each other, so that there were always at least three present. He also changed the commanders frequently. The other Irish troops were camped well back from the barricade and Sarsfield was intent on getting Tyrconnell, who had come to the Irish camp, out of the way. There was a feud between the two men which had its origins in the past – maybe Sarsfield had not forgiven the Viceroy for his advice to James to get out of the country. Anyway, before he left the camp, Tyrconnell, now overweight and ill, gave his advice that the work that stood between the town and the camp should be demolished, according to Stevens:

> His reason was because the garrison might then be continually sustained from the King's army that was hardby, and so far as to be able to drive the enemy out of town though he should have entered, which was undeniably true . . . but Tyrconnell's advice was rejected, I suppose upon a belief that the usual garrison was sufficiently able to hinder the enemy from entering the town . . . Notwithstanding this, St Ruth's confidence was afterwards

> frustrated and the Viceroy's sentiment proved the best and would have proved the preservation of the place. [A]

D'Usson, who had taken command of the fortifications of Athlone, was convinced that it was unnecessary and that the important thing was to stop the enemy from crossing the river. To this end he had blocked up all possible fords and Ginckel was unable to make a pontoon bridge.

The key to Athlone, Ginckel realised, was the bridge. He brought up his artillery and using fascines that his men moved forward to prevent being hurt by enemy fire, his men repaired the bridge with planks. Some grenadiers prepared to dash across, but Sergeant Custume* and some Irish soldiers with axes rushed onto the bridge and cut down the planks. All were killed but twenty men led by a lieutenant completed the work. They too were killed – all bar two, but the bridge was destroyed.

On 28 July, a new attempt was made to repair it, but this time the Irish set the repairs alight and Ginckel was now running out of ideas. Major General Tollemache, pronounced and spelt often as Talmash, was a man who seemed happiest fighting as a soldier. He came up with a daring plan. He would select the tallest men, dress them in front armour,** wade over the river under the bridge, seize the enemy defences, repair the bridge, then the cavalry could take over. MacKay was against the plan, but the Duke of Wurtemberg had three Danish soldiers, all tall men, who had committed some petty crime – probably stealing food from the stores – whom he suggested should try out the ford. They would be spotted by the enemy, said MacKay. We will pretend they are deserters and shoot over their heads, said Tollemache. This plan was carried out and the three men waded over unarmed, but wearing cuirasses, as a rehearsal for the real event. Two were slightly injured, but all three returned and the plan was given the go-ahead.

At 6.00 p.m. the church bells in Leinster town (the Williamite side of the river) rang and the tallest grenadiers, twenty abreast in their cuirasses, led the way, fifteen hundred of them with 'fuses and bags of grenades held over their heads'. The English artillery opened up to keep the Irish from attacking them. For some reason St Ruth had placed the most inexperienced of the Irish regiments in the town under General Maxwell. D'Usson was on the point of entering the town when he was knocked

---

* The Barracks in Athlone are now known as the Custume Barracks.

** The cuirass had largely gone out by 1690, though the Life Guards wore them and Tyrconnell is pictured with one. They had heavy straps over the shoulder to support a backpiece. In this case it seems the Danes only wore the front piece.

down by fleeing troops. The Irish defenders took to their heels. Men rushed over the bridge, Maxwell was captured and the town, seemingly impregnable, was captured in minutes. Hamilton took some reinforcements from the Irish camp to try and re-take it, but he was too late. Ginckel had already manned the walls at the back of the town that Tyrconnell had suggested should have been demolished. Story relates that:

> The rubbish and stuff thrown down by our cannon was much more difficult to climb over than a great part of the enemy's works, which occasioned our soldiers to swear and curse even among the bullets themselves, upon which Major-General Mackay told them that they had more reason to fall upon their knees and thank God for the victory and that they were brave men and the best of men if they would swear less.

Ginckel wrote to the king in England:

> The Count of Nassau, Talmash and Brigadier Bellasyse [showed] great bravery and zeal, cavalry could do nothing. We have taken 2 large and 6 or 7 smaller cannon, a provision of corn and three or four large ovens which we are glad to have. General Maxfield [Maxwell] captive – Cmdr. St Ruth not being in command at the time of attack. 1000 men lost. [E]

The last statement assuredly refers to the enemy. Ginckel had lost some men but nothing like a thousand. It was a fine victory but the Irish army had not been defeated. They had in fact retreated to Aughrim, where they were given ample time to prepare a defensive position. Once again William's army was not good at following up its victories.

8

Aughrim, 12 July 1691

To get an overall picture of the battle of Aughrim, one needs a small plane or helicopter. There are no commanding hills to see the complete battlefield. It is an area of small hills, farms, streams, rocky outcrops and narrow lanes. The main road from Dublin and Ballinasloe crosses Melehan bridge and proceeds over a – in 1691 – very narrow causeway protected by Aughrim Castle. The land to the left is bog for almost two miles until the road from Laurencetown comes in via the Pass of Urraghry to Tristaun ford. The two rivers, the Tristaun and the Melehan, keep the bog land suitably wet even in mid-July and the ridge of Kilcommadan hill with a track running the length of it gave St Ruth and his Jacobite army a considerable advantage. The only small hill for the Williamites was that at Urraghry, to the right of their centre and from there Ginckel, when he arrived, was unable to see more than a part of the battlefield, due to the fog, which did not lift until midday.

After the fall of Athlone, St Ruth's army retired, according to John Stevens in the Grand Prior's regiment, 'in great confusion and disorder'. Men had deserted, especially if they were approaching their own homes and their morale must have been very low. Only Limerick and Galway remained in Jacobite hands. They were running out of space to fight. However, encouraged by their chaplains, every regiment seemed to pull itself together and with four days' grace, before Ginckel, who waited for his artillery ammunition to arrive from Dublin, caught them up, there was time for making individual defensive positions. St Ruth encouraged his infantry to line the hedges so that the enemy would be forced to use only certain approaches which could be well covered. It was a sensible, almost twentieth-century, approach and the Jacobite infantry were to make the most of these tactics. On the right wing, Sarsfield's cavalry defended the Tristaun ford but he was only in charge of his cavalry. The second-in-command was the French General de Tessé, but if de Tessé knew St Ruth's plans, he was not to reveal them later. In command of the Jacobite front line infantry was Major-General Dorrington, lately governor of Limerick and of the second line, Major-General John Hamilton. The ruined Aughrim Castle was defended by two hundred musketeers, with nearby Sheldon's horse and Luttrell's

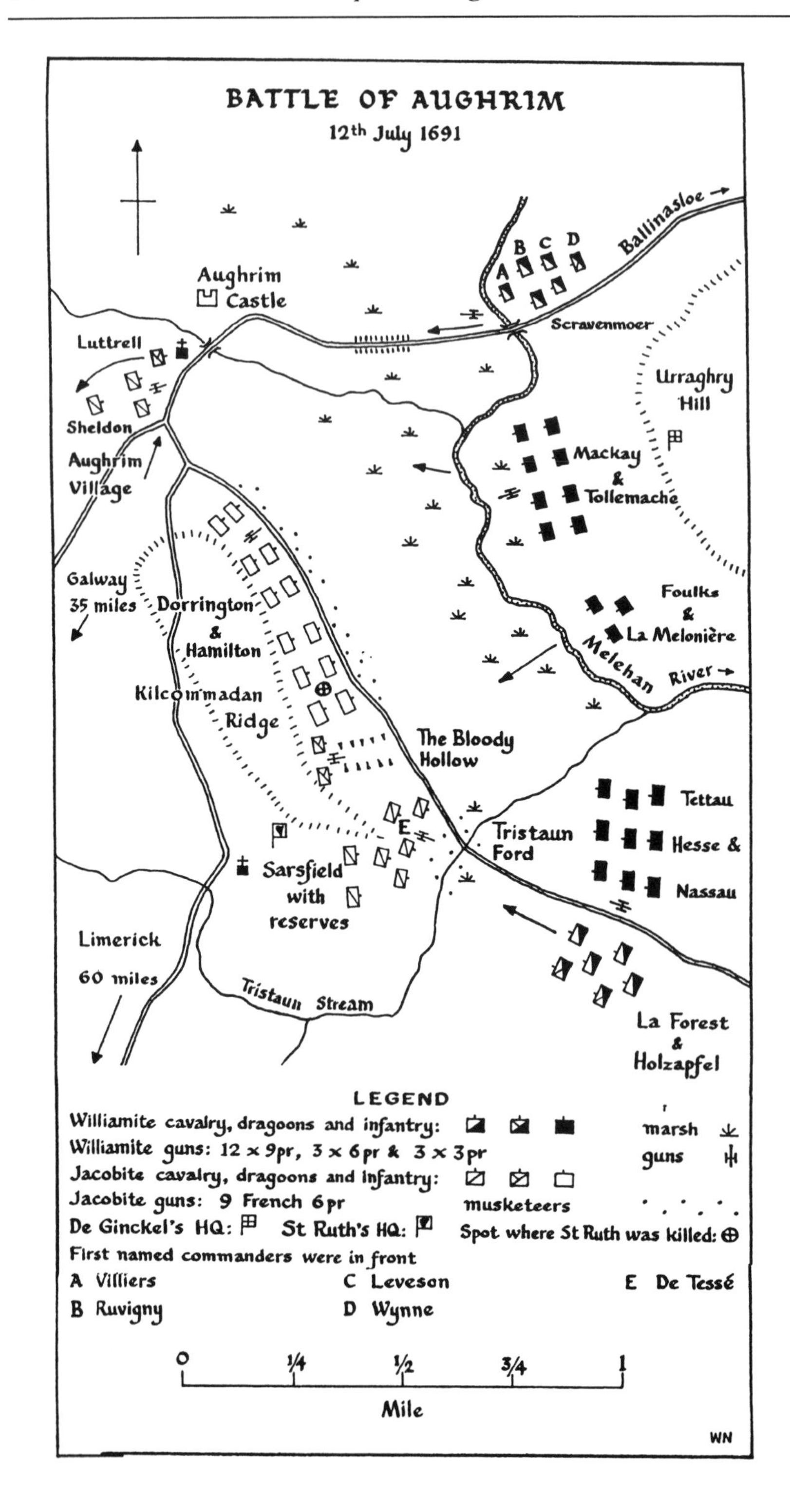
BATTLE OF AUGHRIM
12th July 1691
Aughrim Castle
Luttrell
Sheldon
Aughrim Village
Galway 35 miles
Dorrington & Hamilton
Kilcommadan Ridge
Limerick 60 miles
Tristaun Stream
Sarsfield with reserves
E
The Bloody Hollow
Tristaun Ford
Ballinasloe
A B C D
Scravenmoer
Urraghry Hill
Mackay & Tollemache
Foulks & La Melonière
Melehan River
Tettau
Hesse &
Nassau
La Forest & Holzapfel
LEGEND
Williamite cavalry, dragoons and infantry:
Williamite guns: 12 x 9pr, 3 x 6pr & 3 x 3pr
Jacobite cavalry, dragoons and infantry:
Jacobite guns: 9 French 6pr
De Ginckel's HQ:
St Ruth's HQ:
marsh
guns
musketeers
Spot where St Ruth was killed:
First named commanders were in front
A Villiers
B Ruvigny
C Leveson
D Wynne
E De Tessé
0 1/4 1/2 3/4 1
Mile
WN

dragoons. There were a couple of supporting infantry regiments on this wing.

Ginckel's troops numbered about twenty thousand, (see Appendix B), the same as his opponent but he had more guns and more dragoons. Marlborough's troublesome 'friend', the Duke of Wurtemburg, was his second-in-command. If Marlborough found him difficult, then it is likely the even-tempered Ginckel would. Third in command was General Hugh MacKay, who was in charge of part of the first line of infantry, seven English battalions under Brigadier Bellasyse. Amongst them were Colonel Foulks, of Sedgemoor fame, Kirke, who had been on the king's side at Sedgemoor, Gustavus Hamilton and Lord George Hamilton.

To Mackay's immediate left was Von Tettau and the Danish and French Huguenot foot, with on the wings La Forest and Eppinger's mixture of horse and foot. La Forest was a Huguenot and fought with great courage and tenacity at Aughrim. On the other wing was another newcomer, the Marquis de Ruvigny with the Dutch General Scravenmoer who had assisted Marlborough at the Siege of Cork. They had Leveson and Wynne's horse with Coyningham's horse in the second line. Also in the second line was the redoubtable Colonel Wolsley and to his left Tollemache, Count Nassau and Major-General Holzapfel all commanding seven battalions. Holzapfel had two detachments of cavalry in his line and there were no less than eighteen cannon to which St Ruth had a mere nine in reply.

Ginckel was not in position until 5.00 p.m. when, at MacKay's suggestion, a left-wing attack started for the ford. The rest of the line was kept standing, MacKay awaiting the chance to attack the causeway when some of the enemy troops there were withdrawn. St Ruth had put a sprinkling of dragoons in front of his first line of infantry so as to form a sort of Forlorn Hope. However, things had changed since the civil war and St Ruth's men took advantage of the hedges, stone outcrops and general lie of the land to take up good firing positions and have their horses handy for a speedy retreat when necessary.

Ginckel withdrew Coyningham's dragoons from the right wing and used them to reinforce the Danes and Huguenots on the left. The attack got to the ford and not much further. St Ruth, whose headquarters was near the centre of Kilcommadan hill, had moved over to the church to see what was happening. He now gave orders that some of Sheldon's horse and infantry from the left wing should go to the aid of De Tessé.

Mackay's right wing had stuck. Ordering Gustavus Hamilton and Kirke's infantry over the causeway first, they got to a cornfield and no further. Then Bellasyse and George Hamilton's men crossed and barricaded themselves in near a hedge against Irish cavalry. The infantry of Dorrington and John Hamilton, however, bravely pushed them back and Gordon O'Neill captured a Williamite gun. The position for Mackay was serious. He managed to hold the Irish but an advance was impossible. The left-wing attack was held up because the Irish had defended the ford well. No horse could deploy due to the bog. The reinforcements from each side made it a stalemate.

At about 6 p.m. the regiments of de la Melonière and Foulkes (who had taken over from the wounded Colonel Wolseley) attempted to infiltrate a hollow. The fighting was so fierce here that it became known as the Bloody Hollow.

Men slipped in the mud and their friends following behind fell over them. Cannon fired at close quarters, bodies piled up and the din was too loud for commands to be heard. In all this the Williamite infantry struggled on against fixed Irish defences. They retired to regroup and come on again, regiments mixing with each other. No prisoners were taken here and the wounded were left to fend for themselves. Only when the fighting finished was there an opportunity for dead and wounded to be brought in, the latter being sent to a primitive tent hospital, and the former being buried in mass graves.

Colonel Erle and Herbert's regiments went too far in the middle. Supported by Brewer and Creighton's men they had to cope with the mud as well as the enemy. St Ruth's sharpshooters fired from every hedge, gates were left open for the advance to proceed into fields that were lined with Irish guns, and when these had been forced there was always the Irish cavalry to contend with. Captain Parker, one of the infantry officers complained that:

> We on the right, attacked them, they gave their fire and away they ran to the next ditches and we, scrambling over the first ditch, made after them to the next from where they gave us another scattering fire and away they ran to other ditches behind them . . . here in climbing these ditches and still following them from one to another, no-one can imagine we could possibly keep our order, and here in this hurry there was no less than six battalions so intermingled together we were at a loss what to do. [G]

Story relates that the English infantry was not downhearted:

> The English marched boldly up to their old ground again from whence they had been lately beat; which is only natural to Englishmen, for it is observeable that they are commonly fiercer and bolder after being repulsed than before, and what blunts the courage of all other nations commonly whets theirs; I mean the killing of their fellow-soldiers before their faces. [H]

Aughrim battlefield

The site of Aughrim Castle today

Ginckel had failed to make any headway. He still, however, had his right wing cavalry. He had been aware that St Ruth had taken men from one wing to another to protect the ford. He himself had done the same thing, but Ruvigny and Compton's Blues were not yet in action. The time had come to use them. MacKay was informed and the cavalry formed up two abreast like Cromwell's men at Langport. They had to ride over the causeway only forty feet from the castle, where unknown to them Colonel Burke's men were running short of ammunition and when new ball arrived it was the wrong size for their muskets. Compton's Blues led the way followed by Ruvigny with his horsemen. Luttrell's force gave way. Perhaps Sheldon, who had performed brilliantly at the Boyne, had been transferred to the other wing supporting Sarsfield, but Luttrell, who months later was murdered by someone who suspected him of being in the pay of the enemy, retreated and the route up to St Ruth's position round the back of the Jacobite infantry was open for the Williamite right wing cavalry.

It was at this moment that St Ruth, convinced that he had nearly won the battle, moved out to the top of the ridge, perhaps to collect a fresh body of horse to go to Luttrell's aid. He was killed by a solitary shot from a cannon. Was it the one temporarily captured by Gordon O'Neill? This was not to be the first time that a cannon was captured in battle by someone unable to carry it off or put it out of action. Ney's cavalry at Waterloo over-ran some of Wellington's guns but was unable to do anything with them. Cardigan at Balaclava was in the same position, though he did his best to kill the gunners. One shot however finished the battle for the Jacobites. (See Appendix B.)

de Tessé was unable to stop the successful Ruvigny horse, and himself was wounded. Sarsfield had orders not to move and knew nothing of St Ruth's death. He had Galmoy's horse, so far uncommitted, with him and did his best to cover the retreat to Limerick. The Jacobite infantry that had more than made up for their poor showing at the Boyne, was cut down and only nightfall saved more from being killed. Aughrim Castle surrendered. Of its two hundred defenders, only thirteen officers and forty men survived. All nine guns, forty-four standards, tents and at least four thousand men were lost. The Williamites lost at least two thousand.

Among the Irish prisoners were Gordon O'Neill, Lord Bophin – brother of Lord Galway who was killed – Lords Bellew, Slane and Kenmare and Butler of Kilcash. Story praised the way the Irish had fought. The Guards under Dorrington in particular had leapt over the *chevaux-de-frise*. Colonel Erle, who had commanded his infantry battalion in the centre was captured twice by Irish troops and released when their positions were over-run, was a lucky man. Though wounded, he applied for compensation and was given an extra fourteen days' pay – £16.16s.0d. – for his troubles. Colonel Holzapfel was wounded and the Danes and Huguenots suffered greatly. Colonel Munchgaar, one of the first to cross the Shannon, was killed leading his Danish troops, by a cannon ball like St Ruth.

What would have happened if St Ruth had not been killed? His position was, after two hours fighting, just beginning to be turned and it is likely he would have lost anyway. Macaulay mentions that some of the horse advanced with hurdles which they placed over the bog to get past the worst hold-ups. This was another innovation. Perhaps those who invented the rolled-up runways of World War II had read Macaulay's account of Aughrim. St Ruth had prepared his battle well, but Ginckel was fortunate in his subordinates. They were not prepared to give up; no Williamite considered defeat. The roads to Galway and Limerick were strewn with muskets that had been thrown away by the retreating Irish. Ginckel offered 6d a gun, but soon it was down to 2d a gun and waggon loads were brought into his camp. St Ruth was an unlucky general, who had gambled and lost. Unlike many Jacobite actions, however, everyone knew who was in charge. At the Battle of Sherrifmuir, for example, the Earl of Mar had so many deputies who disagreed with each other that it was almost certain any battle he fought would be a disaster. St Ruth certainly succeeded in installing spirit back into the Irish army; he chose his ground well, his line up was cleverly done. His main mistake was falling out with Sarsfield and not instigating a proper chain of command with de Tessé. The army of Ginckel was quite different. Everyone knew their commander. If Ginckel had been killed, Wurtemburg and MacKay would have taken over. They were going forward, the Irish back. No one knew what would have happened if St Ruth had won but it would only have been a temporary setback for Ginckel who had fresh troops at Athlone and other fortified towns. One of the mysteries is why Sarsfield, the man who had carried out the raid on William's siege train at Ballyneety, was so inactive at both the Boyne and at Aughrim. It seems that he was guarding his king at the Boyne and so took no part in the fight. At Aughrim he seems to have fallen out with St Ruth, who placed him on the right wing in the rear. He was never told to move and only at the end did he attempt to cover the retreat. He has often been pictured as a man of action who did not use his brains to best advantage. This however, is not true: he had dreamt up and carried out the Ballyneety raid and at Limerick it was he, with support from Brigadier Wauchope, who planned to take the Irish army to France. The plan, so strange for William to agree to as it meant they would join Louis' forces against William's in the Netherlands, had to be convincing for Ginckel to agree to it. This surely was Sarsfield's greatest contribution to Irish military history. He created the Wild Geese.

The sudden loss of a commander was not new. It had happened when Old Schomberg had been killed and yet it did not stop King William at the Boyne. This may have been because William was himself in charge and rather ignored his Marshal. St Ruth seems to have made enemies of his fellow officers, but to have been popular with the common soldiers. He had a problem in that he spoke no English, but his main fault was in not communicating his plans before the battle with de Tessé and Sarsfield as well as his other commanders. In 1675 at Sasbach, the French Marshal Turenne had been killed by a cannon ball at a crucial stage in the battle, but old Condé had been rushed to the army from retirement to take over and retrieve the situation. Nothing like this had been possible at Aughrim.

In the Peninsular War the Battle of Corunna had been a British victory, albeit a defensive victory in that the French were kept back, allowing the British army to escape. There, in spite of General Moore's death from a cannon ball, officers knew what to do and the position was held until the fleet sailed. It is easy to blame the general, who was killed, for not instituting a proper chain of command. Why did Sarsfield not take the initiative? He still had some unused cavalry and could have joined with Galmoy and led a counter-charge. De Tessé does not seem to have been a man of initiative, and he had been slightly wounded so was temporarily out of action at the time of St Ruth's death.

There is one other factor in the Irish defeat. Later on, only a few days after Tyrconnell's death in Limerick, Henry Luttrell, commander of the Irish left-wing dragoons, was found guilty of corresponding with Ginckel. Had he deliberately retired because he had been promised something – land, money or both – by Ginckel? He was arrested by D'Usson, commander in Limerick, and would have been executed if Ginckel had not discovered this and threatened to execute the Jacobite prisoners – Dorrington was one – in return.*

There must have been an element of luck on Ginckel's side. A lucky general is usually a good communicator. MacKay seems to think that he was responsible for the victory, but Ruvigny played an equally important part. Ruvigny would not have crossed the causeway without orders to do so from Ginckel. Thus it was a battle that was won or lost by fortune's hand as well as by the sudden and unexpected loss of one commander and the wounding of his second-in-command.

As the Irish escaped to Galway and Limerick, Ginckel once more took up his pen and reported to William:

* Some people never forgave Luttrell and blamed him for losing Aughrim for the Irish. His family became very wealthy but in 1717 Luttrell was shot in his sedan chair in Dublin, not in late vengeance for Aughrim, but by a jealous husband.

> The fight [Aughrim] lasted 4 hours and was very obstinate. The enemy's force was much superior to ours and their position more advantageous. Yet your troops attacked them with the greatest determination and bravery, totally defeating them. Prisoners include Maj-Gen Hamilton, Dorrington & other officers. It is said St Ruth is killed but I have not been able to make sure of it. Maj Gen Holtzapel, Prince of Hesse, Col Cutts and Belcastle are wounded. Nearly 4000 dead lie at the battlefield. The generals of the army have shown the greatest zeal for your service. [E]

He likes the word 'zeal', which appears in both his reports but he certainly doesn't believe in lengthy reports. Like Douglas, he was a general who preferred to direct his troops rather than wield a pen.

Plunket, in *A Light to the Blind,** lists the casualties on the Irish side at Aughrim:

> Amongst the slain was the great General St Ruth, worthy of lasting memory. Next after him the noble youth Lord Bourk (de Burgh), Viscount of Galway, son to the present Earl of Clanrickarde. Brigadier Connel, Brigadier William Mansfield Barker, an English gentleman early killed by a cannonball, Brigadier Henry MacJohn O'Neil, Col.Charles Moore of Kildare, (with his Lieut-Col. and Major), Colonel David Bourk, Colonel Ulrick Bourke, Colonel Constantine Macguire, Col.James Talbot of Templeogue, Colonel Arthur (who had fought valiantly at the Boyne) Colonel Mahony, Lieut-Col Morgan, an English gentleman, Major Purcell, Sir John Everard of Felhard, Col.Felix O'Neill and Dean Alexius Stafford of Wexford, an undaunted zealot and most pious churchman who fell in front of the Royal Regiment as he was encouraging them on the first charge.
>
> There was made prisoners the Lord of Duleek, the Lord of Slane, the Lord of Bophin, (son to the Earl of Clanrickarde), the Lord of Kenmare, Major-General Dorrington, Major-General John Hamilton (who died of wounds in Dublin some three months later), Brigadier Tuite, Colonel Walter Burke, Colonel Gordon O'Neil, Col. Thos Butler of Kilcash, Col. O'Connel, Col. Edmund Madden and several others.

Plunket omits the name of Lord Dillon who was also killed. Most of the wounded who were not captured reached Limerick and those who were captured were released after the treaty of Limerick.

It is said the Williamite forces lost six hundred men, but details are hard

* Nicholas Plunket is the supposed author of *A Light to the Blind – A Jacobite Narrative of the War in Ireland.* This was reissued by J. Gilbert in Dublin in 1892 and is the main source for the Aughrim battle from the Irish side.

to come by. The list of widows claiming benefits for husbands lost is small:

Mary Piggot	£30	Captain of Dragoons	Died Londonderry
Mary Butler	£20	Lieutenant in Beaumont's	Died Ireland
Marg.Hooker	£30	Captain in Herbert's	Died Aughrim
Eliz.Mouse	£20	Lieutenant in Sir M.Bridge's	Died Limerick
Ann Jellett	£20	Lieut. Jellett (Selwyn's)	Died Aughrim
Cornelia Corker	£30	Captain Corker	Died Aughrim
Sarah Carlisle	£30	Captain Carlisle (Wharton's)	Died Aughrim
Jane Adams	£20	Captain Adams	Died of wounds, Ireland

– and only four of them are widows of an officer killed at Aughrim. The list appears in Dalton's Army List for 1690/91/92 and obviously there were some later cases, some unsuccessful. A widow whose husband fell at Steinkirk (August, 1692) had to explain to the authorities that it was her husband who had manned the guns and still she only gets the usual £20 or £30 pension.

The men in Herbert's regiment suffered and Herbert himself vanished and was presumed captured and murdered. Colonel Erle was lucky, twice captured, twice freed, he survived though wounded. The Twelfth Regiment, Wharton's (later the Cheshires) had Major Colt, Captain Carlisle and one ensign killed and seven men wounded which was light compared with the Blues who lost a captain, two lieutenants, one cornet, forty-five men killed and twenty-one wounded. Only Ruvigny's Horse lost more. The Green Book lists the wounded officers as the Prince of Hesse, Lord G. Hamilton, Lord Cutts, Colonel Erle, Lt.Col Brudenell and says that there were seventy-three officers killed and one hundred and eleven wounded.

Colonel Holzapfel was also wounded, as already stated, and one authority says that he died. However, when Ginckel sent his report to King William, Holzapfel was still alive. The Danish officer, Colonel Munchgaar was also killed and Majors Devenish, Petit, Cornwall and Fox with sixty-five other officers. Wounded amounted to nine hundred and six, so it is not surprising that Ginckel paused a while at the battlefield. Pits had to be dug and bodies buried.

In London, John Evelyn writes his diary for 10 July:

> The great victory of King William's army in Ireland was now fresh and looked upon as decisive [the Boyne was not it seems] for the total reduction of that land. The Irish foot had, 'tis said much advantage by being entrenched, but they out-numbered us in horse, but they forsaking the

> foot, a total rout, [many] got slaughtered and loss of all their cannon and baggage followed. The French General St Ruth was slain which deprives them of their best commander; nor was it cheap for us, near 1000 killed but of them 4–5000.

Tyrconnell sent two messages to Louis on 13 July. He sent the Earl of Abercorn in one ship and his secretary Mr Doran in another, with the Duke of Norfolk. He gave each the same message of the disaster at Aughrim, that more troops were needed and instant provisions for Limerick, which he thinks will still be able to hold out. James hoped that Louis would agree to Tyrconnell's request as it was 'Too reasonable not to be complied with' when Norfolk and Doran arrived with the news, Abercorn's ship having been captured en route for France.

The final act of the two-year Irish war was about to start.

9

The Second Siege of Limerick

Before proceeding to Limerick, Ginckel made for Galway. D'Usson was in command here with a force of two thousand five hundred men but Galway was not a defended city. True, D'Usson had six cannon, but both Lord Dillon, who had been governor before D'Usson arrived, and his French colleague realised that the city was not fit for a siege. *A Light to the Blind* reports the situation succinctly:

> On the 18th Galway was invested in which there were seven regiments of foot, not full nor well-armed. Baldarg O'Donnell [a Gaelic leader] was expected with a thousand men, but he came not and took the Prince of Orange's side at the end of the war. On July 19th Ginckel placed a battery against a little new fort which the Irish had made near the town. He took it that same day. Immediately after he raised his batteries against the town. On the 21st the Governor having considered the great declension of Irish affairs, thought it fit not to hold out the place any longer, and so the same day he called for a parley. The treaty was concluded on July 24th whereby the garrison got their own demands . . . On the 26th the Marquis D'Usson went to Limerick, so did Lord Dillon with the garrison.

The Irish were allowed to take their six cannon with them and arms as well. The Irish army at this stage was down to 8,140 infantry, of whom only 3,910 were armed, and 2,400 horse and 2,360 dragoons. The cavalry and dragoons had got away without too much trouble from Aughrim, but the infantry were in a bad way. Lord Kenmare's regiment for example only had 237 sound men out of 800.

Tyrconnell was still in command and one of his last acts was to try Henry Luttrell for treason. Luttrell had been caught in communication with a man called Sebastian, who turned out to be one of Ginckel's officers, about terminating the war. The letter to him was intercepted and read. However, before anything could happen other than his imprisonment the Viceroy was dead, some say poisoned, but before he died, at the age of sixty-one, he left the country in the hands of three civilians: Chancellor Fitton, Sir R. Nagle and a Mr Plowden. Only Nagle was Irish so this did not please the soldiers in Limerick. Berwick describes Tyrconnell as:

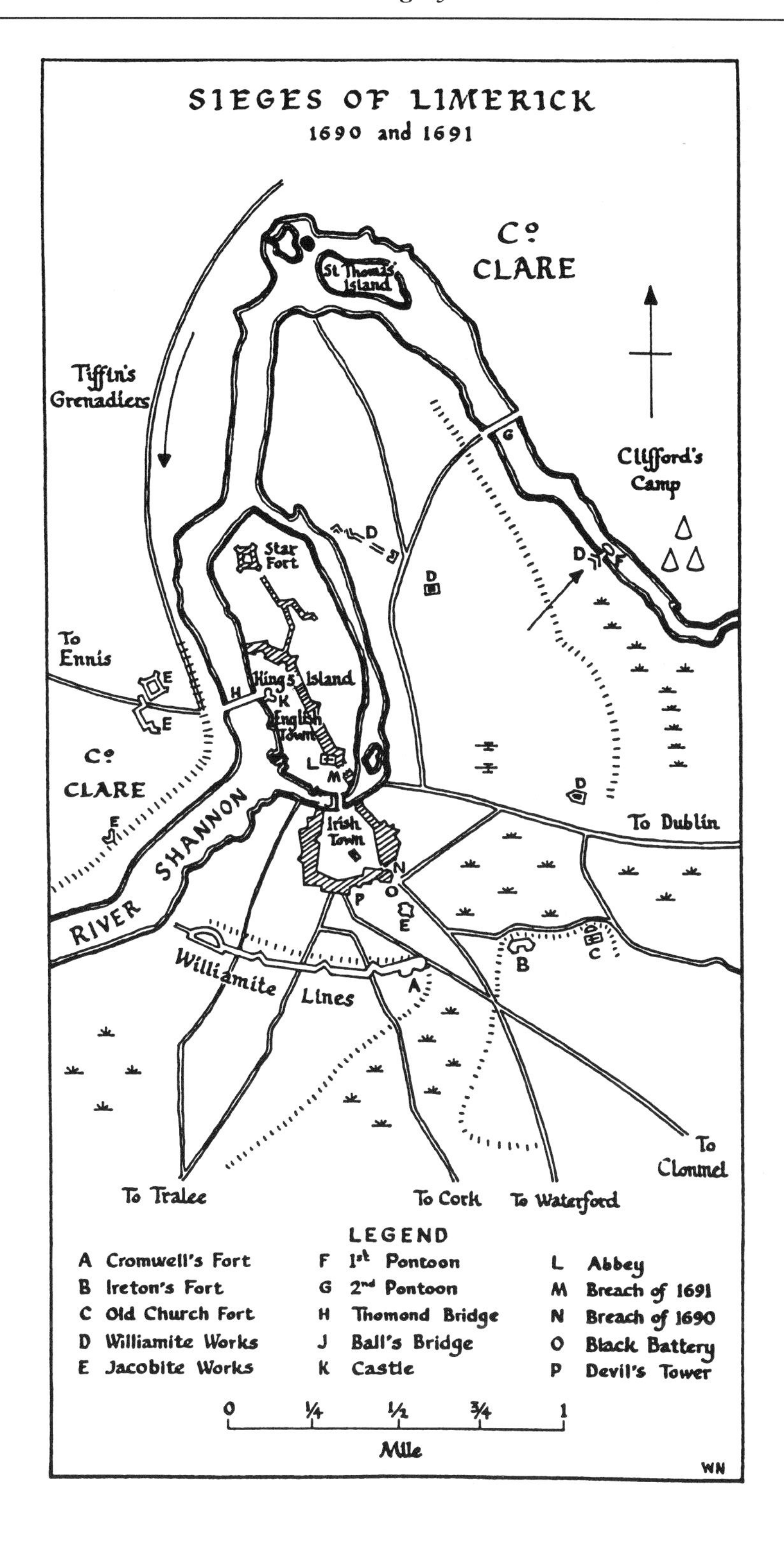
SIEGES OF LIMERICK
1690 and 1691
Co CLARE
St Thomas's Island
Tiffin's Grenadiers
Clifford's Camp
Star Fort
King's Island
English Town
To Ennis
Co CLARE
Irish Town
To Dublin
RIVER SHANNON
Williamite Lines
To Tralee
To Cork
To Waterford
To Clonmel
LEGEND
A Cromwell's Fort
B Ireton's Fort
C Old Church Fort
D Williamite Works
E Jacobite Works
F 1st Pontoon
G 2nd Pontoon
H Thomond Bridge
J Ball's Bridge
K Castle
L Abbey
M Breach of 1691
N Breach of 1690
O Black Battery
P Devil's Tower
0 ¼ ½ ¾ 1
Mile
WN

> A man of very good sense, very obliging, but immoderately vain and full of cunning. He had not a military genius but much courage. From the time of the Boyne he sank prodigiously, being become as irresolute in his mind as unwieldy in his person.

Rumours went round after his death that Tyrconnell had been murdered by his own side. However they may well have been spread by Williamites and it is more likely that the party he had attended at D'Usson's house the night before, the strain of camp life and the war, together with his excessive weight, accounted for his death.

The first siege of Limerick in 1690 had resulted in a clear victory for its French defender. De Boisseleau and his Irish troops had not only kept the attackers out, but strengthened the defences by building a wall within the breach so that Hamilton's troops could not get in. However the real victor of the first siege of Limerick was the weather. It rained so hard that the attackers' trenches filled with water and men were concerned that there would be a situation as at Dundalk camp when so many went down with the flux. The ammunition was short and William was keen to get back to England. The besiegers withdrew in the night and De Boisseleau was left to celebrate a Londonderry in reverse. He wisely spent the time strengthening the walls and outworks as he knew the enemy would return.

The second siege was a different state of affairs. Sarsfield and his cavalry, most of which had escaped the slaughter of Aughrim, were operating in County Clare where there was still fodder for their horses. Ginckel was slow in setting off after Aughrim. He needed fresh ammunition, his men were weary and he needed more food and horses. His attempts to float supplies down the Shannon failed and everything had to come overland from Dublin with large escorts. Inside Limerick, Major-General Wauchope, who had been injured at Athlone and took no part in the Aughrim affair, was in charge of repairing the defences. Ireton's fort was repaired, a new fort built next to it in an old churchyard, and the star fort on King's Island repaired. The Frenchman, de Tessé, nominally in command, was over-ruled by Sarsfield and his council.

In September, when the city was under siege, a paper was passed round – supposedly Tyrconnell's will. It said that both Catholic and Protestant Irish should unite against the French – the Catholic countries of Italy, Germany, Spain and Poland were fighting France. It was a story that certainly had its supporters – had not Lauzun deserted the army immediately after the Boyne? Where were the French ships? It must have made Wauchope and Sarsfield determined to get good terms for their troops. Sarsfield was loyal to James and knew that if James was ever to

View of King John's Castle and Thomond Bridge, Limerick

invade England it would be from France and not from Ireland. He was thinking up a scheme to end the war, which if it succeeded, would be a way of ending the Irish war in one fell swoop.

The ever-cautious Ginckel approached Limerick on 25 August with a plan in mind to make a pontoon bridge out of sight of the town and take his troops round to attack Thomond Bridge. The few fords were well guarded, but Ginckel had twenty-nine tin boats, as well as a siege train of nine 24 pdrs., nine 18 pdrs. and three mortars. Mackay captured Ireton's fort, Nassau captured Cromwell's fort and by 8 September batteries began firing on the town.

On the Clare bank of the city, Colonel Clifford with a mixed force of dragoons and infantry, was responsible for defending the river banks and keeping a special watch on St Thomas' Island, where he had posted forty dragoons. The Williamite engineers were undaunted though and discovered that three small islands further upstream from the main island presented a possibility for a bridge. To get to the first two there were passable fords, then a gap that could be bridged by twenty-five pontoons, where there was a third island with an easy ford to the Clare bank. At night, a party of grenadiers under Brigadier Tiffin was ferried over to the third island, a group of workmen went over with the pontoons, and Scravenmoer with horse and fifteen cannon and Tollemache with five regiments of artillery stood by waiting for the attack.

Brigadier Tiffin led the charge on Clifford's camp. It was an easy target. The luckless defender and most of his men fled to Thomond Bridge and deserted their posts. Sheldon's horse, hearing of the crossing, did not interfere. Tiffin attacked the forts that defended Thomond Bridge. The French major in charge of the drawbridge at the town gate immediately pulled it up leaving about six hundred Irish soldiers to be slaughtered or drowned in the river. Tiffin suffered no more than twenty-five casualties, he captured twenty officers, a hundred men and three brass cannon. Meanwhile the engineers had built a new pontoon bridge so Tiffin was given some reinforcements.

The time had come for Sarsfield's peace treaty and he and Wauchope crossed over to see Ginckel with their seven demands. These were:

1. That their majesties will by an Act of Indemnity pardon all past crimes and offences.

2. Irish estates to be restored to those who possessed them before the revolution.

3. Free liberty of worship and one Priest to each town and parish.

4. Irish Catholics to be capable of bearing employment, military or civil and to exercise professions, trades or callings of what nature soever.

5. The Irish army to be kept on foot, paid, as the rest of His Majesty's forces in case they be willing to serve their Majesties against France or any other enemy. [The spirit of Tyrconnell ruled].

6. Irish Catholics to be allowed to live in towns corporate and cities, to be members of Corporations, to exercise all sorts and manners of trades and to be equal with their fellow Protestants in all privileges, advantages, and immunities accruing in or by the said Corporations.

7. An Act of Parliament to be passed for ratifying and confirming the said Corporations.

The reaction of Ginckel was not surprising, he rejected all terms at once. Burnet said that William had given him secret orders to agree to a peace treaty as soon as possible as the English troops were wanted on the Continent. The French knew that Louis wanted the war to carry on for this reason, to keep them off the Continent. Perhaps this is why they agreed to Sarsfield's rather naïve terms.

Ginckel, with two civilian administrators appointed by William, had drawn up his own treaty. It was divided into a civil one with thirteen articles and a military one with nine articles.

The Treaty of Limerick, duly signed on 3 October, gave Catholics the same liberties they had enjoyed with Charles II according to the laws of Ireland. Free pardon was promised to those who took the oath of allegiance, and they would be allowed to keep their property, bear civilian arms and practise any profession. Those who had opted to go to France were not included in this and there were no specific legal safeguards for Catholic property. There was some trouble over a clause extending terms to people in the counties of Cork, Clare, Mayo, Limerick and Kerry who had been under the protection of the Jacobite army. This clause was not ratified by the Irish Parliament and had to be reinserted by letters patent. The Protestants said the treaty was too easy on the Catholics and vice-versa. The Poynings Law of the fifteenth century, which laid down that all acts of the Irish Parliament had to be approved by the King in London or by his Deputy in Dublin, was not cancelled and would be used by Protestants as a convenience and by Catholics as a grievance.

What was surprising was the clause that permitted the Irish army to be ferried across to France in British ships, the soldiers taking their families with them, to settle on the Continent. They were not allowed to go to Scotland or England. Ginckel had thought some would join his army, by now in need of recruits, but Sarsfield and Wauchope persuaded their men to go to France, saying they would soon be back with a large French army. Only two thousand gave up their arms and went home, one thousand crossed over to their former enemies and the majority, eleven thousand men, went to France to join the French army.

Those who had property in Ireland, especially those with large estates, naturally wanted to stay. The new Earl of Tyrconnell, nephew to the last earl, went with his son to France along with the three advisers appointed by his father. The French squadron under Château-Renault which eventually arrived too late to stop the surrender, was used as a ferry and took the following to France:

Colonels:	23		
Lt. Cols.:	21		
Majors:	45		
Capts.:	230		
Lieuts.:	227		
Ensigns:	246	Total Officers:	792
Private Persons:	29		
Soldiers:	4,726		
Servants (including 130 with French officers)	234	Total:	5,781

Sarsfield had to march with his contingent to Cork. He found thirty-eight merchant ships there for him, and his contingent*

* Total 11,518 men; 4,726 from Limerick + 792 officers and 5,300 from Cork + 700 officers.

embarked but there was not enough space for their wives and families, One report states:

> A woeful sight was seen on the Lee when the transports set sail; Sarsfield had promised the exiles who embarked that their families were to go with them to France. There was no room in the ships to enable the pledge to be fulfilled. Loud cries and lamentations broke out from the wives and children who had been left behind; some dashed into the stream and perished in its depths, some clung to the boats that were making off from the shore; many of the men, husbands or fathers, plunged into the waters; not a few lost their lives in their efforts to reach dry ground. Nevertheless, the mass of our army arrived in France safely. [H]

Special quarters were made available for the men in Brittany and Sir Andrew Lee was sent in December by King Louis to inspect the new arrivals. The first thing he did was to select six hundred of them to make up the deficiencies in the Mountcashel brigade that had come to France before the Boyne.

There were other troops that now joined the Irish in Brittany. Colonel Cannon with his remnants of Dundee's army arrived. The Cork prisoners arrived, or some of them, after a harrowing time. The officers had mostly accompanied Marlborough back to England where they had been shut in the Tower. They were duly sent to Bruges to be exchanged for non-Dutch prisoners in French hands. But the French did not seem to know this and many escaped to Lille where they joined the French army. The soldiers were sent from Cork to Calais where they were later released to join armies in Poland and Saxony. Some no doubt got to France. The number of Irish troops in French service then was about fourteen thousand.

This was divided into:

12,000: Six infantry regiments commanded by Colonels Dorrington, Wauchope, Fitzjames (Lord Prior), Simon Luttrell, Richard Talbot and Gordon O'Neill.

200: Two troops of Horse Guards commanded by Patrick Sarsfield, Earl of Lucan, and the Duke of Berwick.

744: Two regiments of horse under Dominic Sheldon and Lord Galmoy.

Being Irish, there were troops left over. These were merged into the regiments gradually, but some joined the French navy, others the Mountcashel Brigade of three regiments. Nine Irish officers were given command of St Malo privateers.

The army was nominally King James's army and it was to be used to invade England, hence the billeting in Brittany. Louis agreed to this, although he must have wanted to send it to fight in Flanders, Spain and Savoy. In England in early 1692 two Jacobite plotters, Ashton and Cross, were arrested and hanged. James was still relying on the British Navy to defect. James still thought of the sailors as his men. He managed to convince Louis that, as he had been their Admiral, the British navy would not fight against him. By April 1692, all was ready for an invasion. A vast army was commanded by Marshal Bellefonds with de Tessé as second-in-command due to his knowledge of Irish troops. Richard Hamilton, last seen as a captive at the Boyne, was released from the Tower, exchanged for Mountjoy, and commanded the Irish troops with Sarsfield.

The defeat of Tourville at La Hogue put an end to all invasion plans – France had to command the English Channel first and for a hundred years she never managed this, although a small French fleet, commanded by the American Colonel Tate, did succeed in landing nearly two thousand men near Fishguard in 1797.

There were no more transport ships after La Hogue. The Irish troops were distributed to Savoy and Rousillon as well as Flanders where they once more came into contact with the army of King William. Mackay, Mountjoy and Lanier were killed at Steinkirk (August 1692) and at Landen (July 1693) Sarsfield finally took command of the cavalry, when his chief had been wounded, and Berwick had been captured. Leading a charge he was hit by a bullet in the breast and died a few days later in the city of Huy in Belgium.

The terms of the Treaty of Limerick were mostly swept away in the Irish Parliament of 1697 when the Penal Laws were enforced. Some of the land problems had by then been sorted out so this was probably the main success of Limerick. The War of the Grand Alliance drifted on until the Treaty of Ryswick in 1697. The plenipotentiaries could not agree, so William sent his minister, Lord Portland, to see the French general, Boufflers. Three points were put to him: firstly, William wanted James expelled from France, secondly he wanted Louis to give up support of Jacobites and, thirdly, he wanted French Protestants to come and live in the Netherlands. Louis agreed to the first two but disagreed on the third point. James stayed in France but became very taken up with religion and died in 1701. Finally, Louis compromised and agreed to waive the duties on importing goods from Holland so William was placated. The emperor tried to include the Spanish Succession details in the Treaty but the allies refused to allow this and William's coalition of countries known as the League of Augsburg came to an end. For a short while there would be peace.

10

Parliament and the Payment of William's War

The Convention Parliament which met in February 1689 at the same time as King James was setting out for Ireland, was soon beset with the problem of raising money for William's war. At first the Commons were keen to squabble amongst themselves and sort out the relationships between Anglicans and Dissenters. William, short of money, was naturally keen to get onto the important subject of revenue. The bribe of doing away with the unpopular hearth tax ensured his claim to the ordinary revenue but only until 24 June 1689. On 27 February, the Commons agreed 'to stand by and assist the King with their lives and fortunes ... in reducing Ireland' and on the twenty-eighth instigated a bill to raise £420,000 by a six months' assessment on land. Over the next six weeks £600,000 was agreed to be repaid to the Dutch for their part in bringing William to England, £714,000 to Ireland for Schomberg's army, and nearly £1.2 million pounds to the navy for both summer and winter fleets. Still war had not been formally declared with France until John Hampden and Sir Thomas Clarges raised the subject in April and on the sixteenth a motion declaring war was approved.

At the end of April, the Commons voted a poll tax for war money and the ordinary revenue date was pushed on from June to 24 December. A sum of £600,000 was voted for home affairs and £700,000 for the war. This still did not include money to keep Marlborough and his 10,000 men sent to Flanders. Four other means of raising funds were put forward. Firstly, an extra poll tax, then a tax on new buildings in inner London, thirdly a £500 penalty from those who had held office under King James without complying with the Test and Corporation Acts (i.e. Roman Catholics) and finally a new levy on beer and some other drinks. None of these levies, with the exception of the one on beer, came to anything, and it was not until May that Sir Christopher Musgrave proposed a one shilling levy on land, and a toleration bill was passed which effectively put an end to the £500 penalty on Catholics and Dissenters.

In June, the land levy of one shilling became law, but still events, both in Ireland and in the Commons, were not going as quickly as William had expected. In the House of Lords, the Duke of Bolton was conducting an investigation into the conduct of the war. There was also criticism in the

William and Mary: a contemporary plate

Commons about the Dutch. William Bentinck, one of William's closest advisers, later Earl of Portland, was accused of selling places and someone in the Commons pointed out that the Dutch were still trading with France. William was now near despair and considered going back to Holland, leaving Mary to rule in his absence as he thought she would do a better job. He gave notice that before the recess all bills should be completed. Thus three supply bills were passed, and the settling of revenue bill, the famous Bill of Rights, a bill of indemnity, a bill to restore charters and an excise bill were rushed through in a sudden spurt of activity. There was some squabbling between the two houses over Ireland. However, the clause to favour the Hanoverian line if neither Mary nor Anne had any children was passed by thirty-eight votes to twenty-nine at the end of July. The stage had unknowingly been set for the '15 and the '45 Rebellions.

There was still an amount of £600,000 due to the Dutch, which

William said would have enabled them to come to the aid of Torrington at Bantry Bay. The Commons eventually agreed to pay this out of ordinary, not foreign, revenue. The news from Ireland improved things – Londonderry had been relieved, Schomberg had landed, and Waldeck was doing well on the Continent. Once more William faced his parliament. The king asked for more supplies and two Whigs, Sir John Thompson and Sir Thomas Lee, asked for a brief prorogation. This erased bills that were pending and permitted a fresh start. At last, in November 1689, the sum of £2 million was voted for the war in both Ireland and the Continent.

It was all very well voting such huge sums of money, but it had to be decided where it would come from. Half eventually came from the land tax. The other half had to wait. Meanwhile a sum of £50,000 for Princess Anne was voted for the coming year. It seems a great deal, but she was living in style with a huge entourage that included Lady Marlborough.

By early 1690, William had decided to go to Ireland himself and take over the army from the bumbling efforts of Marshal Schomberg. There was a lot of opposition to him going. Halifax recommended a further prorogation of parliament and electing a new one in March. William now suggested to the new parliament that he wanted the ordinary revenue on credit for his Irish war. He was offered the excises, that had been used by both King Charles II and King James II, for the lives of both himself and Queen Mary. But the tunnage and poundage he had expected was only granted for four years. A further £1.2 million was estimated for the 1690 wars in Ireland and the Continent. Only £200,000 of this was expected to be raised by a new poll tax and the rest was to be gathered by loans on the royal revenue.

Thus the financing of William's war was a very hand-to-mouth affair, and the country was not in a very healthy state. Foreigners were unlikely to invest inwardly into a nation that had undergone a revolution. The Indian and West Indian trade brought in some revenue, but re-exports to the Continent were very difficult owing to the war with France. Also the shipping costs were high. Masts and other items came from the Baltic, so that although new ships could be built of English oak, the rigging and cloth for sails came from overseas. The rise of the French privateers, especially after Limerick, did not help the situation and it is even more surprising that the country was able to afford Marlborough's war when it came.

When William finally set sail for Ireland in early June, Mary was left with a council she described as: Carmarthen (Danby): 'of a temper I never can like', Devonshire: 'weak and obstinate', Dorset: 'lazy', Pembroke: 'not very steady', Nottingham, who seemed to have been her chief minister, as: 'suspected by most as not true to the government', Monmouth (Earl of Peterborough): 'mad', Lowther: 'weak', Marlborough, who was on the Ireland committee: 'can never deserve either trust or esteem' – Mary suspected that Lady Marlborough was using her influence with Anne to undermine her court – and even Russell, who took over the fleet from Torrington, 'had faults'.

The success of the Boyne in 1690 was overshadowed by the Battle of Beachy Head and the Teignmouth landing and Bishop Burnet was given to write in October:

> I was never more surprised in my whole life than I am to see the House of Commons in such a [good] temper. [They had just agreed to raise the army to 69,000 men and to £2.3 million to pay for it] All that I know say plainly they dare not go back into their country if they do not give money liberally...in a word the French fleet, by lying so long on our coast, and the King's behaviour in Ireland, as well as King James's meanness, has made so wonderful a change in all men's minds with relation to them both that we seem now not to be the same people that we were a year ago.

Once again to vote large sums of money was causing a problem as to where it should come from. The proposal came to the Commons that one million pounds could come from the sale of forfeited Irish estates. William blocked this but agreed to a commission on accounts being set up. Paul Foley, who had been instrumental in sorting out Schomberg's problems of commissariat with Shales, now took a hand in closely inspecting both naval and army estimates.

The success at Athlone and Aughrim in 1691 helped ministers to meet in a good mood. Lord Carmarthen, often at loggerheads with everyone, had now resigned due to ill-health and Secretary Jephson had died. The fleet estimates nevertheless were cut from the original request of £1,855,000 by £279,000. The army accounts were also closely scrutinised and only £2,101,000 voted for it with a sum of £165,000 to come from the Irish exchequer, whether or not it could afford it.

Men like Robert Harley and Sidney Godolphin were crucial to the government. Both cut their teeth on the finances of 'William's War' as it was called. Other men prospered too in a period when the House of Commons was in a state of change. The Tory party could always be accused of being pro-Jacobite by the Whigs. The latter could be accused of being pro-Dutch by the Tories. The Lords wanted to hang on to their rights and the king's advisors tended to be his close friends like Blaythwayt and Portland. Men like Marlborough were much subject to scrutiny, and yet it was not until after William's death that he came to the fore.

The earl was dismissed from all offices in January 1692, for, according to Burnet, Bishop of Salisbury:

> He had made his peace with King James and was engaged in correspondence with France; it is certain that he was doing all he could to set on a faction in the army and nation against the Dutch and to lessen the King, and that he as well as his wife, who was so absolute a favourite with the Princess, that she (Lady Marlborough) seemed to be the mistress of her whole heart and thoughts, were alienating her both from the King and Queen.

Fortunately for England and the army in particular, the rift did not last for ever. At first, Marlborough became tutor to Anne's son, the Duke of Gloucester, who was born in 1689, and then eventually in 1698 he was restored to the Privy Council. In 1701 he was finally made Ambassador Extraordinary to the Low Countries and Commander of Infantry and Captain General in the forthcoming War of the Spanish Succession.

The history of Irish Jacobitism from 1690 is not one of any note. In 1715 a rising in Scotland ended in the partial Jacobite defeat at Sheriffmuir. The English Jacobites surrendered at Preston. In 1719 a Spanish fleet containing James Sarsfield, son of Patrick, was dispersed by storm before reaching Ireland. A few men landed in Scotland but were defeated by British regular troops at Glenshiel. The Forty-five rebellion in Scotland did not effect Ireland, though four Irishmen accompanied Charles. One, O'Sullivan was his quartermaster and more effectively, another, MacDonnell was the colonel of the Fitzjames Horse who performed well at Culloden Moor in 1746. Most of the Irish troops captured who survived were returned to France in 1747 after a brief imprisonment.

In 1791 the French Revolution caused the organisation, the Society of United Irishmen, to be formed. Protestant and Catholic divisions were cast aside in the effort to free Ireland from government by England. In 1793 the Catholic Relief Bill and the Militia Bill were passed in Ireland so that Catholics could join the Militia. They objected to being forced to do this though. By 1795 a sectarian divide had opened up, the United Irishmen becoming pro-French and pro-Catholic, while the Orange Order and the Ulstermen joined the pro-government forces. In 1798 a small French force under General Humbert arrived and after one success was put down at Ballinamuck. In County Wexford meanwhile the rebel Irishmen were defeated at Vinegar Hill. One of the generals leading troops against them was none other than General John Moore, who some years later achieved both fame and death at Corunna.

Up to 1806 there was a state procession in Dublin to King William's statue on College Green. This was now abolished to avoid hurting Catholic feelings. In Victorian times Gladstone's Home Rule for Ireland bill was defeated in the Commons and rioting broke out in Belfast. The parade celebrating the Boyne in July inflamed the rioteers. In 1890 Col. Waring, a Unionist MP, said that if Gladstone was returned to power a new Tyrconnell would be found in Dublin and all Protestants would be put to death.

The First World War saw many Irishmen, both Protestant and Catholic joining the colours and fighting for Britain. It was a small minority that formed the famous Irish revolt that saw British guns in action in Dublin's streets. The Boyne celebrations were abandoned. In the 1920s both the Boyne monument and the statue of King William in Dublin were blown up, the latter unsuccessfully but it was taken down by the authorities nevertheless.

The Boyne as a political rallying point is still very much in evidence today. There are Orange marches in uniform with banners showing King Billy, and the marchers are not afraid to go through Catholic streets. The police have to try and protect them and get the brickbats from both sides.

The Irish problem is still unsolved and this is being written during the week in 1997 that the Grand National, our greatest horse race, has had to be postponed because of an IRA bomb warning.

What then of the future? At the time of writing the Stormont talks are at a complete standstill and those that have taken place don't seem to have achieved anything. IRA disruption continues and a new ceasefire has not been called.*

Some sort of political decision has to be made and the sooner the better. The children growing up with Irish history must realise that as far as history is concerned the facts are clear. The 'War of the Two Kings', as it is now known, was an extension of the war in Europe. James was fighting for a foothold to cross over and regain his throne in England. William was fighting to put down the opposing forces in Ireland, but he also had an army on the main continent doing the same. It was a continuous struggle against the might of King Louis XIV. It was not a Protestant-v-Catholic, England-v-Ireland war; the fact that it took place in Ireland was simply because James was there. The struggle continued when he went over to France. There were loyal Catholics like Tyrconnell who believed in a Catholic Ireland, but they were not the majority. Men like the Englishman Captain Stevens were fighting for their king,

* At the time of this reprint (April 1998) events had moved forward with results of a Referendum on The Good Friday peace talks awaited.

wherever he was. They were in a minority perhaps and Stevens had to borrow money from a Protestant Dublin friend to exist before he received any pay for being a member of James's army. He was, like Sarsfield, happy to cross over to France after the fall of Limerick and fight again from France.

No easy solution then can lie ahead for Ireland. The hope is with the young people. Many are well-travelled and very well-educated. The age of the terrorist must be in the past, the future has to be more promising. In 1966 Michael MacLiammoir wrote in his book *Ireland*, a statement that maybe sums up the Irish problem:

> The most tragic drawback to my mind is that the Border has momentarily separated, within the confines of one small nation, in the arts, in the world of politics and science and commerce, all Irish energies and their communication. The thought and sympathy and action of what should be a united people have been split into two unequal parts, Dublin and Belfast alone finding themselves, in spite of the negligible distance between them, almost as intellectually divorced, as say, London and Moscow. How long, Oh Lord, how long?

Chronology of Events in the War of the Two Kings 1688–1691

15 November 1688	Landing of William at Torbay with army under Marshal Schomberg.
24 November 1688	Churchill and the Duke of Grafton desert to join William.
11 December 1688	James II flees to France.
18 December 1688	William enters London.
12 March 1689	James II arrives in Kinsale, Ireland with a small Anglo-French army.
1 May 1689	Drawn naval Battle of Bantry Bay.
April–July 1689	Siege of Londonderry.
31 July 1689	Battle of Newtownbutler. William's forces secure the north of Ireland.
August 1689	Schomberg lands at Carrickfergus, captures the castle but goes into winter quarters and loses troops through illness.
14 June 1690	William lands at Carrickfergus with 15,000 men.
30 June 1690	Battle of Beachy Head. French naval victory and the French raid Teignmouth, Devon.
1 July 1690	Battle of the Boyne. William captures Dublin and Jacobites flee to Limerick, Schomberg killed.
2 July 1690	James escapes to France.
August 1690	Sarsfield's raid on the Williamite gun train at Ballyneety.
August–September 1690	First siege of Limerick. William returns to England.
September–October 1690	Marlborough's attack and capture of Cork and Kinsale. Death of Duke of Grafton.
June–July 1691	Siege and capture of Athlone by Williamites.
12 July 1691	Battle of Aughrim. Death of St Ruth, Jacobite commander.
July–August 1691	Second siege of Limerick.

14 August 1691	Death of Tyrconnell.
28 August 1691	Surrender of Jacobites.
September 1691	Treaty of Limerick and Irish soldiers ferried to France.

Appendix A

Story's list of English army present at the Finglas Review on 5 July after the Boyne.

Horse	*Men*
Life Guards 1st/3rd Troops & Horse Grenadiers	368
Oxford's Blues (Royal Horse Guards)	368
Lanier's (1st Dragoon Guards)	360
Villier's (2nd Dragoon Guards)	245
Coy's (5th Dragoon Guards)	236
Byerley's (6th Dragoon Guards)	244
Schomberg's (7th Dragoon Guards)	242
Russell's	242
Langton's (Princess Anne's)	225
Wolseley's (Enniskillen)	423
Harbord's Troop	38
(Harbord was the financial controller and his men were clerks)	
Dragoons	
Hayford's/Matthew's (1st Royal Dragoons)	405
Leveson's (3rd Dragoons – now 3rd Hussars)	246
Wynne's Enniskillen (5th Dragoons, now 5th Royal Lancers)	260
Coyningham's Enniskillen (6th Inniskilling Dragoons)	260
	4,162
Foot	
Douglas' (Scots Guards)	648
Kirke's (2nd Queen's)	666
Trelawney's or Queen's Regiment (4th King's Own)	553
Lloyd's (5th Northumberland Fusiliers)	652
Babington's (6th Royal Warwickshire)	416
Beaumont's (8th King's, Liverpool)	526
Stuart's (9th Norfolk)	660
Hanmer's (11th Devonshires)	593

Brewer's/Wharton's (12th Suffolk)	571	
Hastings' (13th Somerset Light Infantry)	606	
Meath's (18th Royal Irish)	678	
Gus Hamilton's (20th Lancashire Fusiliers)	560	
Bellasyse's (22nd Cheshire)	628	
Herbert's (23rd Royal Welsh Fusiliers)	600	
Deering's (24th South Welsh Fusiliers)	600	
Tiffin's Enniskillen (27th Royal Irish Fusiliers)	625	
Fowke's (with Matthews – see Dragoons – he was one of Monmouth's colonels in Sedgemoor Campaign)	439	
Lisburne's	611	
Earle's	693	
Mitchelburne's	664	
St John's (Londonderry Foot)	584	
Drogheda's	660	
Geo Hamilton's	583	
White's (ex – Walker's Londonderry Foot)	600	
Hamilton's	600	
	15,416	
French Huguenots H.395, F 2231	2,626	
Dutch Horse	1,683	
Foot	3,704	
Dragoons	621	
Danes: Horse	812	
Danes: Foot	4,581	
Foreign Troops:	14,027	
Plus: 1,700 officers & sergeants (Foot)		
1,200 officers & sergeants (Horse)	Total:	2,900
Add: 300 Horse killed/missing		
700 Foot killed/missing	Total:	1,000
Strength of William's army:		37,505

Appendix B

AUGHRIM

The Line of Battle 12 July 1691
William's army
(Based on Harvey's *History of 5th Lancers*)

MAJOR-GENERALS

La Forest   Tettan   MacKay   Scravenmoer

BRIGADIERS

Eppinger   La Melonière   Bellasyse   Villiers

1st Line

[Leveson (3rd D.G.)
[WYNNE (5th Lan. 2 squad.)
[Oxford (Blues)
[Langston
[Ruvigny
[Villiers (and D.G.)

[Kirk (2nd Foot)
[Gus. Hamilton (20th Foot)
[Herbert (23rd Foot)
[Lord G. Hamilton
[Ffoulks
[Bellasyse (22nd Foot)
[Brewer (12th Foot)

[La Melonière
[Du Cambon
[Belcastell
[Greben
[Danish Foot
[Danish Foot
[Danish Foot

[La Forest's Dragoons
[Schested
[Donep
[Boncourt
[Montpouillon
[Eppinger

MAJOR-GENERALS

Holzapfel   Nassau   Tollemache   Ruvigny

BRIGADIERS

Schak   Prince of Hesse   Stuart   Leveson

2nd Line

[Coyningham (6th Drag.)
[WYNNE (5th Lan. 1 squad.)
[Lanier (2 D.G.)
[Wolseley
[Byerley (6th D.G.)

[Stuart (9th Foot)
[Erle (19th Foot)
[Tiffin (27th Foot)
[Crighton
[St. Johns
[Lisburn
[Meath (18th Foot)

[Nassau Regiment
[Lloyd (6th Foot)
[Cutts
[Danish Foot
[Danish Foot
[Danish Foot
[

[Schak's Dragoons
[Neiuhense Dragoons
[Zuhistern Dragoons
[Reidesell Dragoons
[Ginckel Dragoons
[Eppinger Dragoons

J R Harvey has used Grant's plan of the Williamite line-up at Aughrim to show that the 5th Lancers were in both the front and second lines. In fact, there were changes in the progress of the battle. Coyningham's dragoons were rushed to help Eppinger. Herbert's and Erle's regiments charged together in the middle with help from Crichton. Ffoulks and La Melonière teamed up with the other Huguenot foot regiments. Wolseley had been shot in the stomach in a minor engagement in May, and was not present, so his second-in-command would have been in charge of his horse.

There is no mention of Ginckel and his deputy, the Duke of Wurtemburg, or the artillery. Ginckel was in close touch with MacKay during the battle, so would probably have been on Urraghy Hill surrounded by his aides.

THE ARTILLERY AT AUGHRIM

The exact position of the gun that killed St Ruth is unknown. Brigadier K A Timbers of of the Royal Artillery Institution has written to me about this and I quote his letter:

> I have to say that the maximum range for most of the guns you mention was considerably greater than the normal fighting range of about 800–1,000 yards. At this latter range, guns were fired using richochet from the ground, aiming to keep the ball skipping across the ground at below head height. At this type of practice, it meant that a lot of the gun's potential range was scrubbed off by the ricochet action as well as by the low trajectory. But if the gun was elevated to any reasonable angle – say up to five degrees of elevation – the range was considerably greater, and the distance you mention was easily achievable. In theory, of course, the gun would achieve its maximum range (in vacuo) at 45 degrees, but this was never used because the target would have been out of sight! If there was poor ground in the area of the target, the gunners would quickly have switched from ricochet fire to direct engagement – it would have been an automatic reaction by any gunner who saw that his fire was being affected by boggy ground.
>
> Whether or not the gunners concerned in this case were aiming at St Ruth is not for me to say! Taking his head off would have been a lucky shot, but I never cease to be surprised at what could be achieved with a smoothbore gun in those days. Some of the shooting was uncannily accurate, given the materials to hand.

The Irish historian, Dr Murtagh, has said that:

> A 3 pdr or 6 pdr could fire effectively up to 500 metres and 12 and 24 pdrs up to 1,000 metres. Maximum ranges of four to five kilometres (i.e. over half a mile) were possible but the ball would have negligible velocity at point of impact (it would kill someone though).

The Green Book gives an unlikely Irish story about the affair. Firstly, the author says that it was a 6 pdr gun that did the damage and it was raised on planks. He gives a folklore account of a herdsman, O'Kelly, seeking redress the day before the battle for the Irish army eating some of his sheep. St Ruth refused his claim, saying he should be hanged. He even refused to give him the skins, as his men were using them at night to keep warm. The determined O'Kelly then went to a cavalry officer in Ginckel's army who, on the day of the battle, took him to Captain Trench and his 6 pdr cannon. This was lined up on St Ruth's quarters and O'Kelly gave the command to shoot, but not before Trench had removed a boot to steady the gun. 'I see his hat fly off' said O'Kelly, 'and his head is in it.' The weakness of this story is that St Ruth was not in his headquarters when he was killed and also it is unlikely that a cavalry officer would have time to escort an Irish shepherd, who may have been a spy, to one of his artillery officers. There would no doubt have been problems of communication. However, it is a good story.

Appendix C

JACOBITE ARMY

The British Museum Add MS 9763 lists the Roll Call of the Jacobite Army in October, 1689, which is reprinted here as it appears in *A Light to the Blind.* The French officer who compiled it had difficulty with Irish names and more than one spelling often appears for the same soldier.

NOTES

Estat Major:	Officer on General Staff
Ayde-major:	Adjutant or carrying out the duties thereof.
Maréchal des logis:	One who helped with the quarter-mastering, positioning of tents, supplies of both food and ammunition, feeding horses etc.
Aumosnier:	Chaplain
Chirurgien:	Surgeon
Réformé:	Wounded, or not available for fighting.
Tambour major:	Drum major
A la suitte:	Following, i.e. officers attached to a regiment but not yet allocated a squadron or platoon.

The totals come to approximately:

Infantry officers:	1,807	Men:	29,354
Cavalry/Dragoons officers:	475	Men:	5,438
Total:	2,282		34,792
Less Mountcashel's Brigade sent to France, approx:			
(officers)	400	Men:	6,300
Less in Cork and other garrisons, approx:	350	Men:	6,000
	750		12,300
Total left for the Boyne:	1,632		22,492

With so many names being the same – the MacMahon Regiment has 13 Reillies and 11 MacMahons – it must have been a nightmare for the roll-call. The wonder is that the French could get such an accurate picture of the Jacobite army. The Guards were under Colonel Dorrington (foot guards) and the Horse Guards were divided between the Duke of Berwick and Patrick Sarsfield. At the Boyne Berwick's 200 or so fought very bravely and Sarfield's horse escorted the king off the battlefield and took no part in the fighting.

JACOBITE ARMY IN IRELAND, 1689
ESTAT DE TROUPES DE ROY D'ANGLETERRE EN IRLANDE, 1689

INFANTERIE

Régiment d'Antrim

Noms des Capitaines	*Lieutenants*	*Enseignes*	*Sergents et soldats*
Antrim, colonel	Magdaniel	Purcell	47
Talbot, lieut.- colonel	Magdaniel	Makay	57
Magrah	Magdaniel	Magdaniel	29
Magdaniel	Shiel	–	59
Rosly	Shiel	Tuly	38
Maguennis	Sauvage	Roy	39
Briguouel	Power	Bryen	44
Magdaniel	Magmanus	Magdaniel	46
Ter: O'Neil	Sixton	Magmahon	50
O'Neil	Macdaniel	O'Neil	54
Burk	Macdaniel	Burk	50
Vaghan	Moore	Vaghan	36
12	12	11	549

Estat major: – Monsieur le comte d'Antrim, colonel. – Talbot, lieutenant-colonel. – Shiel, major. – Calaghan, ayde major. – Macault, chirurgien. – Herault, aumosnier.

Officier à la suitte du dit régiment: le sieur Alexandre MacDaniel, capitaine.

Régiment de Boisseleau

Capitaines	*Lieutenants*	*Enseignes*	*Hommes effectifs*
Duret, Grenadier	De la Martiniere, Rouville	–	52
M. Boisseleau	Barry	Cott	105
Beaupré	Mahony	Gould	54
Barry	Barry	Daly	53
Fitz Gerald	Fitz Gerald	Magrah	46
Buttler	Butler	Tridle	41
Trant	Trant	Barry	37
Suiny	Suiny	Suiny	45
Hide	Roch	Glory	50

Capitaines	*Lieutenants*	*Enseignes*	*Hommes effectifs*
Cogan	Barry	Macartie	48
Barret	Macartie	Macartie	57
Flo: Macartie	Gorman	O'Donoghue	46
Cal: Macartie	Macartie	Gran	36
Fitz Gerald	Guin	White	55
Bryan	Condon	Barry	49
Macartie	Macartie	Macartie	45
Trant	Trant	Barret	44
Swyny	Roche	Keefe	50
Dorny	Harold	Garnan	38
Fitz Gerald	Galloay	Fitz Gerald	43
W Fitz Gerald	Macmahon	Stack	45
Lery	Galloay	Swyny	41
Courcy	Courtin	Keefe	49
M Dhoquincourt	Butler	Carty	43
Luis	Bryan	Fitz Gerald	59
Hurly	Stapleton	Hurly	55
26	27	25	1286

Estat major: – M. de Boisseleau, colonel. – M. de Beaupré, lieutenant-colonel. – M. Macartie, major. – M. Fitzgerald, M. Falwey, ayde majors. – M. Mumer, M. Guiev, maréchaux des logis. – M. David, M. Quilin, aumosniers. – M.Bryan, M. de Beulle, chirurgiens.

Officiers à la suitte du régiment: – Capitaines François: Darpentigny, De Sainte Marie, Du Cerf, La Pierre, De Joux, Du Vignaux, Boucault, La Vauge, cadet. Capitaines Irlandois: Courtin, Falwey, Cotte. Lieutenants François: St Phale, Broues, La Porte. Lieutenants Irlandois, Baggot, Pierce.

Régiment d'Edouard Butler

Capitaines	*Lieutenants*	*Enseignes*	*Hommes effectifs*
M. Butler, colonel	Butler	Burk	58
Hency, lieut.-colonel	Sheau	Sheau	55
My Lord Montgaret	Rafto	Lego	51
Butler	Butler	Jacqueman	40
Aylward	Forstal	Yvers	68
J Fitz Patrick	Fitz Patrick	Fitz Patrick	44
Fitz Patrick	Purcel	Fitz Patrick	57
Power	Power	Magrah	36
Nolan	Marchal	Nolan	50
Blancheville	Leigh	Daniel	55

Capitaines	*Lieutenants*	*Enseignes*	*Hommes effectifs*
Baron	Dormer	Buttler	39
Pay	Pay	Boyton	48
Bishop	William	Kees	47
Comins	Ahern	Shean	47
14	14	14	746

Estat major: Monsieur Butler, colonel. – Henecy, lieutenant-colonel. – Deluau, Lieutenant-colonel François. – Le sieur Goghagan, major. – Williams, ayde-major. – Bourdon, maréchal des logis. – Le Père Jean, Capucin, aumosnier, – Hagan, chirurgien

Officiers à la suitte du régiment: – Capitaines François: Bachelier, Dumesny. Capitaines Irlandois: Henecy, Taafe.

Régiment de Richard Butler

Capitaines	*Lieutenants*	*Enseignes*	*Hommes effectifs*
Fort, grenadier	{Kelly} {Fitz Gerald}	–	35
M. Butler, colonel	Carny	Buttler	54
Archer	St Leger	Fitz Gerald	28
Buttler, senior	Sutton	Raguet	32
Fitz-Haris	Rayan	Stafford	40
Doran	Roch	Kern	36
Kelly	Kelly	Kelly	22
Buttler	Mandeville	Newport	30
Buttler, junior	Fourde	–	29
Lincoln	Boulger	Walsh	29
Sexton	Cokely	Jordan	41
Fitz Gerald	Fitz Gerald	Langton	42
Buttler, lieut.-colonel	Buttler	Fagan	26
13	14	11	444

Estat major: – M.Buttler, colonel. – M.Buttler, lieutenant-colonel. – M. Desbordes, François, lieutenant-colonel. – M. Buttler, major. – M. Buttler, ayde-major. – M. Kelly, maréchal des logis. – M. Kelly, chirurgien. – Père Morphy, aumosnier. – M. McKennins, Capitaine à la suitte. – M. Dupost, lieutenant François.

Régiment de my lord Bedlew [Bellew]

Capitaines	*Lieutenants*	*Enseignes*	*Hommes effectifs compris sergents*
Lucas, grenadier	Alpen et Clinton	–	57
My Lord Belleu	Le Sieur Belleu	Lay	68
Thomas Beller	Macardel	Pipard	67
Pippard	Barnewal	Lay	58
Clinton	Clinton	Clinton	50
Val.Roussel	Roussel	Hennelan	46
André Roussel	Clinton	Delahaye	53
Morphy	Morphy	Morphy	52
Rich.Belleu	Belleu	Doudal	40
Owen Morphy	Morphy	Crowly	47
Jean Hannelan	Hennelan	Hennelan	42
C.Hennelan	Vacante	Hennelan	45
MaKenna	MaKenna	Farel	48
W.Roussel	Carol	Carol	52
O'Neil	Vacante	Morphy	35
Pa.Bellew	Craly	Doudal	58
Fitz Gerald, Lieut.-col	Knowels	Ardel	60
17	17	17	878

Estat major: My lord Belleu, colonel. – Le sieur Fitz Gerald, lieutenant-colonel. – Le sieur Doudal, major. – Le sieur Artane, ayde-major. – Melan, maréchal des logis. – Père Kelly, aumosnier. – Taafe, Chirurgien.

Officiers à la suitte du dit régiment: – De la Cour, capitaine François. – Roussel, capitaine.

Régiment de Bagnel

Capitaines	*Lieutenants*	*Enseignes*	*Hommes effectifs compris sergents*
Duyer, grenadier	Buttler et Buttler	–	10
Bagnel, colonel	Bourk	Comerfort	42
[O] Brian	O'Brian	Lenan	46
Hogan	Maurice	Hogan	33
Moclar	Tobin	Moclar	27
Power	Wadding	Power	25
Prendergast	Prendergast	Blakenig	38
Magher	Magher	O'Bryan	26
Gaffeney	–	Bourk	36
Roche	Prendergast	Ketin	63
Pourcell	Dwyer	Purcell	63

Capitaines	*Lieutenants*	*Enseignes*	*Hommes effectifs compris sergents*
Fannin	Connor	Betrige	38
Power	Power	Power	68
13	12	12	515

Estat major: – Le sieur Bagnel, colonel. – Le Sieur Power, lieutenant-colonel. – Le sieur Corbet, major. – Le sieur Tobin, ayde-major. – Doherty, maréchal des logis. – Begly, aumosnier. – Tobin, chirurgien.

Régiment de Thomas Buttler

Capitaines	*Lieutenants*	*Enseignes*	*Soldats et sergents*
Coulovray, grenadier	{Hacquet} {Mahus}	Lieu-} tenants}	37
Thomas Buttler	Barry	Tobin	38
Jean Buttler	Smit	Tobin	10
D'Autel	Sarsfield	Mandevil	34
Jacques Buttler	Buttler	Burk	41
Bryen	Ouly	Comerfort	39
Lambert	Quirk	Harsdecken	28
Shea	Malon	Tobin	38
Prendergast	Tobin	Faril	29
Kehoer	Comerfort	Luker	39
Delaroche	Tobin	Roche	39
Mandeville	Mandeville	Mandice	30
Neugent	Mandeville	Mandeville	26
13	14	12	428

Estat major: – Mr. Thomas Buttler, colonel. – Mr Wattson, lieutenant-colonel. – Price, major. – Maher, ayde-maior. – Kendy, maréchal des logis. – Folou, aumosnier. – Fauuit, chirurgien.

Officers à la suitte de ce régiment: – Dufay, capitaine, – Tuvuy, capitaine. – Linch, Lieutenant.

Régiment de Nicholas Browne

Capitaines	*Lieutenants*	*Enseignes*	*Hommes effectifs*
Morphy, grenadier	Donaghue et Morphy	–	68
Mr Brown, colonel	Mac Aulife	Macartie	68
Traps, lieutenant-colonel	Calahane	Grady	66
Mac Aulife	Mac Aulife	Gould	68
Callaghan	Callahan	Callaghan	68
Grady	Browne	Riordan	68
Barry	Barry	Desmond	68
Ferreters	Macartie	Rice	67
O'Keefe	O'Keefe	Tewhie	68
Fitz Gerald	Hayes	Riordan	68
Lombard	Keaghly	MaCartie	68
Jacques Fitz Gerald	Roche	Elliot	68
Heas	Leary	Heas	68
13	13	12	881

Estat major: – Mr. Browne, colonel. – Mr. Trapps, lieutenant-colonel. – Mr. Mccaulife, major. – Macaulige, ayde-major. – Daly, maréchal des logis. – Brown, aumosnier. – Callanan, chirurgien. – Tambour major: Better.

Régiment de Barrett

Capitaines	*Lieutenants*	*Enseignes*	*Hommes effectifs*
Jean Roche, grenadier.	Swyny, Buttler	–	56
Barret, colonel	Nagle, Barry	Donovant	59
Hensy, lieutenant-colonel	Calanan	Callanan	28
Roche	Roche	Keary	54
Fitten	Fitz Gerald	Gould	55
Meade	Keefe	Barry	45
Couchin	Barry	Couchin	53
Barry	Barry	Macarty	48
R.Barry	Barry	Barry	48
J.Barret	Condon	Barret	53
Elliot	Buttler	Goran	49
Henecy	Magrah	Wealan	49
Heffy	Roch	Daniel	55
13	13	12	652

Estat major: – Jean Barret, colonel. – Richard Hennessy, lieutenant-colonel. – Jean Roche, major. – Thomas Carew, ayde-major. – Edmond Barrett, maréchal des logis. – Calanane, aumosnier. – Fran: Hanglin, chirurgien.

Régiment de Bophin

Capitaines	*Lieutenants*	*Enseignes*
Wich, grenadier	–	–
My lord Bophin, colonel	Burk	Maddin
French	French	French
Brown	Kelin	Macdaniel
Kelly	Kelly	Kelly
Linch	Blake	Maddin
Burk	Flaharty	Merick
Capitaines	Lieutenants	Enseignes
Linch	Ouaringh	Killin
Flaherty	Flaherty	Flaherty
Martin	Martin	Martin
Burk	Burk	Burk
Burk	Burk	Linch
Blake	Blake	Linche
13	12	12

Estat major: – My lord Bophin, [colonel] – Mahony, lieutenant-colonel – Boissin, major. – Maddin, ayde-major. – Gilles, capitaine réformé. – Lasemby, lieutenant réformé. – Bahir, enseigne. – Dolnin, aumosnier. – Sbiré, chirurgien. – Higny, quartier-maître.

Régiment de Dominick Browne

Capitaines	*Lieutenants*	*Enseignes*	*Hommes effectifs*
D. Browne, colonel	Browne	Bodkin	68
Tho. Linch, lieut-colonel	Linch	Gallagher	64
Jean Blake	Martin French	Skerret	68
Farrogh McDaniel, grénadier	O'Daniell, O'Connel	–	65
François Martin	Browne	Tho. Frinche	62
Mat: Frinch	Dom: Linch	Pa: Frinche	58
Andrew Nowlan	Mat: Linch	W.Skerret	58
Gregoire Frinch	Nich: Frinch	Gregoire Joyce	59
An: Athey	G. Burk	Tho. Athey	61
Jacq: Darcy	François Dorsy	F. Dorsy	61
Chris: Frinch	Jacq: Blake	D. Frinch	61
Pierre Linch	Val. Blake	P. Moris	68
D. O'Connor	M. O'Connor	Terence O'Connor	68
13	13	12	821

Estat major: – Mr Browne, colonel. – Mr Linche, lieutenant-colonel. --, major. – D. Browne, ayde-major. – Henry Browne, aumosnier. – Lennan, quartier-maître. – Gorcy, chirurgien.

Régiment de Clancartie

Capitaines	*Lieutenants*	*Enseignes*	*Hommes effectifs*
Macartie, grenadier	Keefe, Macartie	–	11
My [lord] Clancartie	–	Macartie	25
Rycaut	Talbot	Mac Henry	22
Hall	Copinger	Daniel	13
Power	Calahan	Charleton	23
Swyny	Condon	Fitz Gerard	18
Purcell	Moore	Creagh	26
–	Fitz Gerald	Quigly	29
Morphy	–	Desty	17
Callaghan	Barry	Burn	29
Fitz Gerald	Darington	Daly	17
McDonah	McThus	Makarty	19
Skelton, lieut. colonel	Condon	Fitz Gerald	0
12	11	12	269

Estat major: – My lord Clancartie, colonel. – Skelton, lieutenant-colonel. – Ricault, major. – Moore, ayde-major. – Condon, maréchal des logis. – Conner, chirurgien. – Le père Hegartie, aumosnier.

Régiment de Creagh

Capitaines	*Lieutenants*	*Enseignes*	*Hommes effectifs*
Dowde, grenadier	Plunket, Hanlan	–	38
Sieur [Michael] Creagh, colonel	Molon	Plunket	51
Diermont	Evrard	Diermont	53
Pa[le]s	Bedlot	Bourk	57
Purcell	St Isane	Fitz Maurice	41
Bellieu	Brown	Kelly	42
Fagan	Craan	Evrard	39
La Roche	Eustace	Conner	42
Warren	Hadzer	Hadzer	41
Hins	Bellieu	Bourk	48
Sutton	Archbold	Foster	47
Buttler	Bryan	Kery	45
Dalton	Brown	Dalton	51
Power	Laplante	Congly	40
14	14	13	633

Estat major: – le chevalier Creagh, colonel. – Mr Power, lieutenant-colonel. – Mr Bourk, major. – Mr Plunket, ayde-major. – Mr Fagan, aumosnier. – Hogan, chirurgien. – Mahony, maréchal des logis.

Officers à la suitte de ce régiment: – Capitaines Irlandois: Carny, Jourdan, Brown. Capitaines François: Charmont des Rocher, Sarazin, Dionemont, Dassy, La Broue. Lieutenants François: Fontenelle, Louveau.

Régiment de Clanrickard

Capitaines	*Lieutenants*	*Enseignes*	*Hommes effectifs et sergents*
Talbot, grenadier	Mahon et Hurst	–	43
My lord Clanrickard, colonel	Jean Burk	Lally	56
Madin, lieutenant-colonel	Linch	Madin	58
Crofton	Daly	Connor	56
Daly	Kelly	Coningane	58
Burk	Daly	Kelly	56
Stephenson	Madin	Burk	56
Bermingham	Burk	Bodkin	59
Dorsy	Dowde	Fitz Maurice	45
Daly	Burk	Mileady	62
French	French	Hopkins	52
Faril	Bermingham	Taufe	67
Dowde	Flaharty	Dowde	63
13	13	12	735

Estat major : – My lord Clanrickard, colonel. – Le sieur Madin, lieutenant-colonel. – Le sieur Mariener, lieutenant-colonel François. – Le sieur Bermingham, major. – Le sieur Myleady, ayde-major. – Le sieur Mahon, quartier-maître. – Le sieur Burk, aumosnier. – Le sieur Neulan, chirurgien.

Régiment de Cormocke O'Neale

Capitaines	*Lieutenants*	*Enseignes*	*Nombre des soldats*
O'Neale, grenadier	Maginis, O'Mahon	–	38
Cormock O'Neale, colonel	O'Cane	Macanully	38
Felix O'Neale, lieutenant-colonel	Walsh	Cahanry	63
O'Hagan	O'Neale	Cane	50
Stuart	Stuart	Stuart	30
Magnaghten	Mackay	Magnaghten	31
Cahan	MacDaniel	O'Cane	41
Con. O'Neale	Magonzinan	Macnamée	52
Gilmor	Gilmor	Magil	50
Cormock O'Hagan	O'Hagan	O'Hagan	50
Mac Vegh	Neale	Neale	48
Art O'Hagan	C.O'Hagan	C. O'Hagan	31

Capitaines	*Lieutenants*	*Enseignes*	*Nombre des soldats*
Dobin	Dobin	Dobin	44
Gribin	Flemin	Shyel	29
B.O'Neale	Macanry	Maconmy	46
Rice	Rice	Neale	45
Cor: O'Neale	Magin	Macory	48
J. O'Hagan	Hagan	Hagan	45
A. O'Heara	Heara	Heara	51
Da O'Hagan	Hagan	Hagan	36
Con O'Neale	MacVegh	Hagan	51
Clement	Gardner	Trayner	49
Neale O'Neale	O'Neale	Macrowly	51
Jacques O'Neale	O'Neale (vacant)	Crowly	51
Buttler	Dohorty	Dohorty	52
Maquillin	Macquillin	Macquillin	56
Hegartie	Dowgan	Hegartie	51
A. O'Hagan	Hagan	Hagan	46
28	27	27	1273

Estat major: – Cormock O'Neale, colonel. – Felix O'Neale, lieutenant-colonel. – MacDaniel, major. – Flemin, ayde-major. – Crowly, quartier-maître,.- Neale, aumosnier. – Dobin, chirurgien.

Régiment de Cavenagh

Capitaines	*Lieutenants*	*Enseignes*	*Hommes effectifs*
Ignace Cavenagh, grenadier	Booth et Fisher	–	47
Cavenagh, colonel	Kinslagh	Cavenagh	59
Lacy, lieutenant-colonel	Brown	Raquet	50
Symon Cavenagh	Burne	Ja: Burne	52
Eustace	Eustace	Fitzgerald	55
Nickson	–	Nickson	40
Ed. Cavenagh	Kinsella	Weade	63
Esmond	Cavenagh	Vacante	62
Walsh	Ivers	Walshe	40
Fitz Gerald	Gattaka	Burne	56
Warren	Archbold	Vacante	36
Nolan, Capitaine	Douygent	Burne	39
12	11	9	599

Estat major: – Cavenagh, colonel. – Lacy, lieutenant-colonel. – Deveraude, major. – Weade, ayde-major. – Fisher, maréchal des logis. – Kinselagh, aumosnier. – Magrah, chirurgien.

Officiers à la suitte du dit régiment: – Capitaines François: Edmar, Du Fossé, Dattantat.

Régiment de Clair à Cork

Capitaines	*Lieutenants*	*Enseignes*	*Hommes effectifs*
Skiddy, grenadier	Skiddy, Kenedy	–	–
My lord Clare	Courard	Fitz Gerald	–
Arthur, lieut.-colonel	Burk	Burk	–
Rowe	O'Brien	Mansfield	–
Callahan	Callaghan	Bourk	–
Roche	Callaghan	Stritche	–
Ryan	Ryan	Tubbes	–
Lacy	Lacy	Lacy	–
O'Brien	Egane	Barleigh	–
Barry	Lane	Bourk	–
Harrold	Creagh	Harrold	–
Rawleigh	Samson	Rawleigh	–
Carol	Ryan	Macnamee	
13	14	12	–

Estat-major: – Mr Dillon, colonel. – Bork, lieutenant-colonel. – Dalton, ayde-major. – Dophin, maréchal des logis, – Dillon, aumosnier. – Dignai, chirurgien.

Officiers à la suitte: – Dillon, capitaine. – Linch, capitaine. – Maguire, lieutenant, – Knip, lieutenant-enseigne. – Flaharty, sergent.

Régiment de Maurice Eustace

Capitaines	*Lieutenants*	*Enseignes*	*Hommes effectifs*
Jacques Eustace, grenadier	Archbold, Toull	–	43
Le Chevalier Eustace, colonel	Browne	Eustace	58
Fitzpatrice	Kelly	Favell	47
Allin	Casert	Lalin	48
Eustace	Kelly	Gouldin	49
Tho.Fitz Gerald	Fitz Gerald	Fitz Gerald	51
Maurice Fitz Gerald	Fitz Gerald	Madruder	46
Linch	–	Hart	31
Eustace	Betteford	–	39
Eustace	Fitz Gerald	Cusacq	40
Archbold	Raftorne	Eustace	39
Charlocque	–	Sherlocque	42
Morphy	Houuraine	–	29
Davis	Daevis	Lawlesse	33

Capitaines	*Lieutenants*	*Enseignes*	*Hommes effectifs*
Cognan	Fitz Gerald	Fitz Gerald	45
Segreffe	–	Degane	32
Fitz Gerard	–		46
17	13	13	783

Estat major: – Le chevallier Eustace, colonel. – Le sieur Vaugaud, lieutenant-colonel. – Le sieur Fitz Patrice, major. – Fitz Eustace, ayde-major. – Fitz Gerald, quartier-maître. – Fitz Gerald, aumosnier. --, chirurgien.

Officier à la suitte de la régiment: – Dufais, capitaine. – Dupectaille, capitaine. – Tiché, lieutenant. – St Brimot, lieutenant. – Du Torville, lieutenant.

Régiment de Fitz Gerald

Capitaines	*Lieutenants*	*Enseignes*	*Hommes effectifs*
Magrah, grenadier	Hiky, Laroche	–	77
Le Chevalier Fitz Gerald	Lacy	Comin	51
Stapleton	Stephenson	Kenedy	39
Girardin	Piquot	Brien	51
Bagot	Barry	Bagot	44
O'Keefe	Lacy	Calahan	32
Nugent	Antonin	Yong	53
Roch	Gibbon	Connell	60
Bourk	Garvan	Lacy	65
Girardin	Lavally	Callahan	61
Gibbon	Shea	Arbott	40
Maurice	Sulevan	Harbert	48
Creagh	Maguire	Owenle	17
13	14	12	638

Estat major: – Le Chevalier Fitz Gerald, colonel. – Jean Beengi, lieutenant-colonel. – Stapleton, lieutenant-colonel. – Fitz Gerald, major. – Rawly, maréchal des logis. – Le père Fingé, aumosnier. – Mac Donnogh, chirurgien.

Officier à la suitte du dit régiment: Rawly, capitaine.

Régiment des Gardes-Corps

Noms des Capitaines	*Lieutenants*	*Enseignes*	*Sergents et soldats*
Arundel, grenadier	Rourk, Nolan et Caral	–	87
Darington, colonel	Bourk, Kelly, Houquet	Salter	89
Rouste	Cliton, Nolan	Arthur	75
Doudal	Wefort, Magdaniel	Archbold	79
Mahony	Lally, Grace	Kenely	86
Linch	Kenely, Christophle	Cusacq	85
Robers	Plonket, Madin	Kimptorne	72
Haket	Nihil, Taafe	Magdaniel	83
Dungan	Waris, Pourcell	Plunket	71
Arthur	Dassigny, Rayen	Dillon	76
Barker, lieut. colonel	Comerfort, Gouny	Storton	79
Talbot	Edouard, Hauen	Terwirt	75
Helmer	Tiper, Sheldon	Helmer	76
Segry	Davis, Mouloy	Tif	71
Haston	Rayen, Brenan	Barnoel	74
Waler	Dillon, Dalton	Plonket, Comin	66
Roussel	Roussel, Carney	Chamerlain	87
Doudal	Woldon, Linch	Plonket	75
Tuite	Warin, Hill	Meade	77
Latton, grenadier	Cusacq, Toul	Hogan	81
20	36	19	1564

Estat major: – Darington, colonel. – Parker, lieutenant-colonel. – Le sieur Arthur, major. – Bourk, ayde-major. – Realy, autre ayde-major. --, maréchal des logis. – Hasmard, chirurgien major. – Deux ausmoniers.

Officiers à la suitte: – Fax, lieutenant. – Houquet, enseigne. – Taafe, enseigne.

Régiment de Gormanston

Capitaines	*Lieutenants*	*Enseignes*	*Soldats*
Geraldin, grenadier	Faril, Geraldin	–	42
Gormanston	Preston	Dillon	42
Dorsy	Barnewal	Plonket	33
Guernan	Carol	Meriman	56
Pierre Barnewal	Warin	Stokes	32
Darcy	Don	Roger Guernon	38
Huger Guerlan	Dorsy	Tho, Guerlan	35
Crom	Rosly	King	25
Hussy	Stokes	Haris	32
Bietagh	Bietal	Bietal	52
Hacquet	Dillon	Taafe	52
Mathew Barnewal	Jacq. Hoger	Manin	50
Holmer	Bourk	Warin	35
Eustace, lieut.colonel	Preston	Born	54
14	14	13	578

Estat major: – My lord Gormanston, colonel. – Eustace, lieutenant-colonel. – La Montade, autre lieutenant colonel. – Geraldin, major. – Doun, ayde-major. -- , maréchal des logis. – --, chirurgien. – -- l'aumosnier.

Régiment de Grace

Capitaines	*Lieutenants*	*Enseignes*	*Hommes effectifs sergents compris*
Kadan	Person, Kadan	–	38
Grace, colonel	Grace	Day	55
Moore	Short	Hogan	48
Walsh	Dalton	Faril	54
Ro: Grace	Grace	Grace	55
Chivers	Connor	Farril	52
O. Grace	Kenedy	Kenedy	42
Hore	Carny	Bryen	46
Browne	Dalton	Gibbons	48
Pay	Morphy	Morphy	15
Dalton	Grace	Dalton	27
Brenan	Brenan	Archdeacon	42
12	12	11	580

Estat major: – Mr Grace, colonel. – Le sieur Grace, lieutenant-colonel. – Le Sieur Moore, major. – Le sieur Person, ayde-major. – Le sieur Kenedy, maréchal des logis. – Martial, aumosnier. – Martin, chirurgien.

Régiment de Gallway

Capitaines	*Lieutenants*	*Enseignes*	*Hommes effectifs*
My lord Gallway	Sulevan	Caroll	42
Power	Stapleton	Chevan	62
Burk	Burk	Burk	30
Power	Burk	Power	33
Lally	Lally	Lacy	31
Dalton	Burk	Vacante	48
Dillon	Flaharty	Math	61
Horan	Wolverston	Fitz Patrick	44
Ulick Burk	Burk	Linch	35
Carol et Magrah	Artekin et Magrah	Horan et Hogan (deux compagnies jointes)	46
Donolan	Burk	Richeson	27
M. Burk	Atkins	Hogan	45
Flaherty, lieut-colonel	Linch	Maly	26
13	13	14	530
		Plus: centneuf arrivés après la revue:	109
			639

Estat major: – My lord Galloway, colonel. – Le sieur Flaharty, lieutenant-colonel – Le sieur de St Ville, major. – Le sieur Calaghan, – Le sieur Burk, maréchal des logis. – Le sieur Dillon, aumosnier. – Le sieur Taafe, chirurgien.

Deschamps, capitaine François à la suitte du dit régiment.

Régiment de Hamilton

Capitaines	*Lieutenants*	*Enseignes*	*Hommes effectifs*
Plonket	–	–	–
Duprat	Plunket, Doyle	–	8
Hamilton, colonel	–	Chief	34
Cestreville	Amgurly	Faril	31
Gibbons	Ford	Guilvirne	41
Morphy	Doffe	Sanders	33
Standly	Arffes	–	31
Bouloutone	Plonket	–	20
Harlocque	Harlocque	Hououraine	36
O'Hara	O'Hara	O'Hara	46
Trois	Magué	Ford	30
Nugent	Hagan	Maginis	54
12	10	8	364

Estat major: – Mr Hamilton, colonel. – le sieur Nugent, lieutenant-colonel. Le sieur Talbot, major. – Le sieur Magny, ayde-major. – Le Gaagane, quartier-maître. – Kelly, aumosnier., chirurgien.

Officiers à la suitte du dit régiment: – Le sieur Setick, capitaine. – Le sieur Couloureign, –. – Le sieur Houuraine, lieutenant. – Le sieur Ford, enseigne.

Régiment de Kilmallock

Capitaines	*Lieutenants*	*Enseignes*	*Hommes effectifs*
Barsaba, grenadier	Martin et Terry	–	53
My [lord] Kilmallock, colonel	Terry	Hurly	40
Power, lieutenant-colonel	Power	Power	47
Buttler	Buttler	Buttler	44
Roche	Buttler	Savage	48
Bermingham	Griffin	Fitz-Gerald	55
Egan	Din	Egan	47
Noble	Noble	Kelly	46
O'Daniel	Swyny	Dohorty	57
Ed. Fitz Gerald	Spencer	Fitz Gerald	46
Jacq. Fitz Gerald	Nihil	Dorsy	48
Burk	Johnings	Mark	49
Jacq. Power	Power	Power	41
Garet Fitz Gerald	Fagan	Morphy	51
Gallwey	Power	Gallwey	48
15	15	14	720

My lord Kilmalock, colonel présent. – Le sieur Power, lieutenant-colonel présent. – Le sieur Coulange, lieutenant-colonel. – Le sieur Chapel, major. – Le sieur Nihil, ayde-major. – Le sieur Dohorty, maréchal des logis. – Le sieur Cantillon, aumosnier. – Le sieur Mahony, chirurgien.

A la suitte: Capitaines: Le sieur Nerault, le sieur St Germain.

Régiment de Kilmare [Kenmare]

Capitaines	*Lieutenants*	*Enseignes*	*Hommes effectifs*
Le Chevalier Hurly, grenadier	Bryan et Meade	–	61
My lord Kilmare [Kenmare], colonel	Pierce	Jean Power	60
Morphy	Archer	Callahan	58
Archdeacon	Plonket	Goulde	55
Browne	Roche	Mahony	59
Macaulife	Morphy	Macaulife	61
Macmahon	Wolf	Douly	68
Barret	Barret	Barret	67
Moore	Goulde	Nagle	54
Rives	Quarter	Ozié	58
Cantwell	Doner	Cantwel	64
O'Connor	Magdaniel	Magdaniel	68
Trant, lieutenant-colonel	Macgillycuddy	Macgillycuddy	63
13	14	12	796

Estat major: – My lord Kilmare [Kenmare], colonel. – Le sieur Trant, lieutenant-colonel, p[résent]. – Le sieur Morphy, major. – Le sieur Gibbon, ayde-major. – Le sieur -, quartier-maître. – Reilly, aumosnier. —, chirurgien p[résent].

Régiment de Louth

Capitaines	*Lieutenants*	*Enseignes*	*Hommes effectifs*
Chris: Plunket, grenadier	Plunket et Moore	–	36
My lord Lowth, colonel	Ma: Plunket	Thomas Plunket	59
George Fitz Gerald, lieutenant-colonel	Fitz Gerald	Fox	20
Silvestre Plunket	Edmond Plunket	Ch. Plunket	49
R.Bedlew	Bedlew	Doudal	57
Jacques Plunket	Edm. Donolan	Mapis	49
Babe	Babe	Babe	43
J. Archer	R. Archer	Vacante	41
Donalan	Kelly	Davis	67
Mic. Plunket	M. Kerwan	Kelly	45
Taafe	Flemin	O. O'Neale	46
Trogmorton	Bedlew	Brett	48
R.Plunket	Luke Plunket	Walter Plunket	43
13	13	12	603

Estat major: – My lord Louth, colonel. – George Fitz Gerald, lieutenant-colonel. –

Rossillon, premier major. – Le sieur Plunket, second major. Flemin, ayde-major. – Brady, aumosnier. – O.Plunket, maréchal des logis. – Jean Cassidy, chirurgien.

Officiers à la suitte du dit régiment: – Capitaines: Le sieur Goutaille, le sieur Beauchapelle, le sieur Moudion; le sieur Jennings, enseigne.

Régiment de Mont Cashell

Capitaines	*Lieutenants*	*Enseignes*	*Hommes effectifs*
Hogan, des grenadiers	O'Brien et Macartie	–	19
My lord Mountcashel, colonel	Vacante	Treulee	21
Macartie	Fitz Gerald	Macartie	16
Ivorie	Carol	Lavallin	9
Vacante	Sulevan	Fitz Gerald	17
Brown	Hogan	Macartie	20
Duly	Macarty	Molvany	29
G. Fitz Gerald, v:	Swyny	Lalesse	19
Vacante	Maurice	Kouet	21
Roth	Chivers	Roth	25
Meaghir	Cusack	Comin	31
Power	Vacante	Colgraue	20
Condon	Condon	Callaghan	64
Brien	Rayne	Rayne	60
13	12	13	395

Estat major: – My lord Mount Cashell, colonel. – Le sieur Colgraue, lieutenant-colonel. – Le sieur Panhouet, lieutenant-colonel en second. – Le sieur Roth, major. – Le sieur Hogan, autre-major. – Le sieur Meaghir, ayde-major. – Le sieur Marchand, maréchal des logis. – Burk, aumosnier. – Owens, chirurgien.

Régiment de Macartymore

Capitaines	*Lieutenants*	*Enseignes*	*Hommes effectifs*
Donnoghue, grenadier	{Donoghue} {Donoghue}	–	45
Macartymore, colonel	Gibbons	Macarty	37
Macarty, lieut. colonel	Herault	Mahony	39
Feris	Macdaniel	Melefont	30
Ed.Barry	Barry	Dermot Holahan	37
Roche	Sulevan	Roche	28
David Barry	Barry	Madin	33
Burk	Maguire	Burk	35
Fitz Gerald	Fitz Gerald	Fitz Gerald	25
Morrogh	Gould	Carew	46
Macarty	Terry	Terry	34
Mac Swyny	Macarty	Gorman	20
Driscoll	Macartie	Macarty	42
13	13	12	451
		Plus: 69 hommes arrivés des malades, etc.	69
			520
		Plus: des malades	43
			563

Estat major : – Macartymore, colonel. – Macarty, lieutenant-colonel. – O'Brien, major. – Mahony, ayde-major. – Gould, maréchal des logis. – Macouxin, aumosnier. – Magra, chirurgien.

Régiment de Macmahon

Capitaines	*Lieutenants*	*Enseignes*	*Hommes effectifs*
Macmahon, colonel	Macmahon	Kinelagh	68
Reily, lieutenant-colonel	Ward	Macmahon	68
Hugh Magennis	Con. Magenn[i]s	Burn	68
Pa: Macmahon	Jacques Duffy	Felix Duffy	68
Miles Reily	Philippe Reily	Brady	68
Connor Reily	Edmond Reily	Bryen Reyly	68
Charles Reyly	Th. Reyly	Pa: Macmahon	68
Esmond Reily	Hugh Reily	Philippe Reyly	66
Hugh Reily	Tho. Reily	John Reily	68
Jean Brady	Philippe Brady	Pa: Brady	67
Duffy	Macmahon	Duffy	68
Coll: Macmahon	Edm: Macmahon	Syl: Macmahon	68
Pa: Macmahon	Macmahon	Owen Macmahon	68
13	13	13	881

Estat major: – Macmahon, colonel, – Reyly, lieutenant-colonel. – Macmahon, major. – Connelly, ayde-major. -- , maréchal des logis. --, aumosnier. – Macmahon, chirurgien.

Régiment de Mac Elligot

Capitaines	*Lieutenants*	*Enseignes*	*Hommes effectifs*
Macarty, grenadier	Macowdall et Dowling	–	54
Mac Elligot, colonel	Macfinin	Macarty	61
Hussey, lieut.-colonel	Harding	Conow	66
O'Donoghue	O'Donoghue	Macarty	51
Fitz Gerald	Ja : Fitz Gerald	Mac Elligot	62
Macgillycuddy	Mac Jones	Macgillycuddy	47
Stephenson	Mich : Stephenson	Maurice	66
Charles Mac Carty	Owen Macarty	Sulevan	60
Jean Fitz Gerald	Fitz Maurice	N. Fitz Gerald	66
Owen McCarthy	O'Donnoghue	Callaghan	66
Aylmer	Aylmer	Conner	62
Feriter	Rice	Feriter	63
Fitzmaurice	Tho: Elligot	Val. Elligot	69
13	13	12	793

Estat major: – Mac Elligot, colonel. – Hussey, lieutenant-colonel. – Major, vacante. – Cahasy, ayde-major. – Sale, maréchal des logis. – Pierse, chirurgien. – Gloster, aumosnier.

Régiment de Moore

Capitaines	*Lieutenants*	*Enseignes*	*Hommes effectifs*
Moore, colonel	–	-	78
-, lieutenant-colonel	–	-	65
François Don	–	-	72
Caroll	–	-	51
Wolverston	–	-	51
Chorlock	–	-	50
Burne	–	-	46
Grace	–	-	57
Anthony	–	-	68
Terence Don	–	-	58
Brenan	–	-	44
Daniel Don	–	-	59
Jean Connor	–	-	44
Joseph Birne	–	-	51
14			794

Estat major: – Mr. Moore, colonel. --, lieutenant-colonel. – Bourk, major. – Pourdon, ayde-major. – Cantlon, quartier [-maître]. – Moulan, aumosnier. – Seamor, chirurgien. – Haris, lieutenant á la suitte du dit régiment.

Régiment de Nugent

Capitaines	*Lieutenants*	*Enseignes*	*Hommes effectifs*
Nugent, colonel	Neugent	Nugent	48
Tho. Nugent	Grady	Metresson	49
Miledy	Dalton	Burk	57
Nagle	Goghagan	Iky	52
Plonket	Nugent	Kenedy	53
Ma: Nugent	Horlestan	Warren	38
Misset	Doudal	Dais	60
Robert Nugent	Faril	Rely	26
Dais	Nugent	Fais	41
Fais	Fais	Nugent	49
Faril	Faril	Nugent	48
Robert Nugent	Nugent	Nugent	47
Nugent, lieut.-colonel	Tyrel	Petit	57
13	13	13	625
	Plus : trente quatre hommes de recrues		34
			659

Estat major : – Mr. Nugent, colonel. – Mr. Nugent, lieutenant-colonel. – Le sieur Baker, major. – Le sieur Maguy, ayde-major. – Le sieur Nugent, maréchal des logis. – Le sieur Fisemond, aumosnier. – Le sieur Doudal, chirurgien.

Officers à la suitte de ce régiment: – Mr. Delapanouse, lieutenant-colonel François. – Le sieur Bourde, capitaine. – Le sieur Maguy, capitaine. – Le sieur Beharly, capitaine. – Le sieur Radais, le sieur Prendre, lieutenants François. – Le sieur Hourlestan, enseigne.

Régiment d'Oxburgh

Capitaines	*Lieutenants*	*Enseignes*	*Hommes effectifs*
Oxburgh, colonel	Carol	Moore	25
Scot, lieutenant-colonel	Scot	Conner	25
Oxburgh	Donnel	Ash	30
Pay	Mouloy	Everard	27
Carol	Carol	Carol	61
Coghlan	Moloy	Comerfort	56
Daly	Chanly	Daly	40
Dulhanty	Dulhanty	Dulhanty	40
Flatry	Coghlan	Duigin	21
Connor	Donal	Connor	39
Moony	Moony	Coghlan à Athlone	64
Maddin	Callanan	Callanane	58
Dowling	Dowling	Kelly	65
13	13	13	551

Estat major: – M. Oxbourgh, colonel. – M. Scot, lieutenant-colonel. – M. Dulhanty, major. – Mouloy, ayde-major. – Tobin, maréchal des logis. – Parlan, chirurgien. – Kelly, aumosnier.

Officiers à la suitte du dit régiment: – Capitaines: Macarty, Goutridge, Mouloy. – Lieutenant: Molunan. -Sergent: Coghlan.

Régiment d' Ogara
[Blank]

Capitaines	*Lieutenants*	*Enseignes*	*Hommes effectifs*
Nelan, grenadier	Hurly and White	–	72
O'Brien, colonel	Macnamara	Macnamara	72
La Motte Darquet, lieutenant-colonel	Burk	White	63
Denis Obrien	Sales	Hear	71
MacMahon	Barry	Bourk	69
Sarsfield	Cannan	Sarsfield	66
Moulouny	Moulouny	Striche	69
Ryan	Comins	Ryan	69
Callaghan	Bridgeman	Calaghan	68
Macnamara	Dwyer	Dod	69
Magrah	Hehar	Burk	70
Connel	Barry	Connel	68
Macnamara	Macnamara	Grady	68
Mahony	Macdonogh	Macmahon	68
14	15	13	962

Estat major: – M. Obrien, colonel. – Le sieur la Motte Darquet, lieutenant-colonel. – Le sieur Saxby, major. – Le sieur Nicholas Comin, ayde-major. – Le sieur De Bourgo, quartier-maître. – Le père Hurly, aumosnier. – Le sieur Bolton, chirurgien.

Régiment de Gordon O'Neale

Capitaines	*Lieutenants*	*Enseignes*	*Hommes effectifs*
Gordon O'Neale, colonel	O'Neale	O'Neale	30
-, lieutenant-colonel	–	-	36
Robert Stuart	–	-	38
Arthur O'Neale	–	-	27
Mackan	–	-	30
Jean O'Neale	–	-	38
Hugh O'Cahane	–	-	33
Conn O'Neale	–	-	21
Jean O'Cahan	–	-	33
O'Daniel	–	-	24
Danely	–	-	32
John O'Neale	–	-	29
Maguire	–	-	17
Turlogh O'Neale	–	-	37
14			425

Estat major: – Gordon O'Neale, colonel. – Con: O'Neale, lieutenant-colonel. – Henry O'Neale, major. – Adam O'Cahan, ayde-major. – Carbery, chirurgien. – Anthonie Daly, aumosnier. – De la Sabliere, capitaine réformé. – Deschamps, capitaine réformé.

Régiment O'Donovan
[Blank]

Régiment du Grand Prieur

Capitaines	*Lieutenants*	*Enseignes*	*Hommes effectifs*
Osmond, grenadier	Holar et Eustace	–	38
My lord Grand Prieur, [colonel]	Kenedy	Barnewal	26
Le sieur Clincham, lieut.-colonel	Grace	Rigny	34
Moore	King	Wolverston	20
Usher	Usher	Grace	32
Ugan	Duquit	Bryen	22
Savage	Dobin	Musehy	37
Nugent	Stephens	Reade	29
Macmahon	Macmahon	Maginis	34
Roirk	Roirk	Roirk	60
Talbot	Mortimer	Conway	18
Rodesbye	Cavellier	Vacante	15
Sutton	Bedlew	Morgan	26
Kindelan	Neale	Kindelan	50
Sherlock	Develin	Pursell	30
Tyrel	Donbelliere	Tyrel	43
MacSwyny	MacSwyny	Dohorty	49
McGauran	–	-	49
Walsh	Keating	Neale	47
Obrien	Vacante	Obrien	59
Dempsy	–	Don	36
21	19	18	754

Estat major: – My lord Grand Prieur, colonel. – Le sieur Clinchamp, lieutenant-colonel. – Nugent, major. – Le sieur Develin, ayde-major. – Le sieur Neale, quartier-maître. – Le sieur Neale, aumosnier. – Kennedy, chirurgien.

Officers à la suitte du régiment du Grand Prieur: – Capitaines: Le sieur Cauvin, le sieur Bellignie, le sieur Arnold, le sieur Cordore, le sieur Panton, le sieur Barnes, le sieur Teiling, le sieur Belson, le sieur Adams, le sieur Justy, le sieur Knightly, le sieur Callanane. Lieutenants: Le sieur Blackburne, le sieur Ricardée, le sieur Kendrick, le sieur Pedly, le sieur White. Enseignes: Le sieur Borré, le sieur Munson.

Régiment de Reyly

Capitaines	*Lieutenants*	*Enseignes*	*Hommes effectifs*
Edmond Reyly, grenadier	Reyly Rady	–	47
Ed. Reyly, colonel	–	-	–
Luke Reyly, lieutenant-colonel	N. Smith	Ph. Reyly	67
Jean Reyly	Edm. Reyly	Jean Reyly	65
Fitz Patrice	Fitz Patrice	Fitz Patrice	56
Bryan Reyly	Charles Reyly	Owen Reyly	60
Macabe	Macabe	Reyly	62
Edm. Reyly	Jacq. Reyly	Charles Reyly	56
Jean Reyly, senior	Brian Reyly	Charles Reyly	67
Jean Reyly	Owen Reyly	Bryan Reyly	56
Owen Brady	Tho. Brady	Jacq. Brady	52
Kernan	Kernan	Kernan	52
Jean Reyly	Owen Reyly	Edm. Reyly	66
Jean Reyly	Jacques Reyly	Hugh Reyly	62
Charles Reyly	Edm. Reyly	Daly	58
Jacq. Reyly	Owen Reyly	Owen Reyly	66
Smith	Smith	Smith	60
Nicho: Smith	Ed : Smith	Tho. Smith	62
Hugh Reyly	M. Reyly	Daly	58
Edm. Reyly	Art. Calan	Tho. Reyly	31
20	19	18	1103

Estat major: – Monsieur Edmond Reyly, colonel. – Luke Reyly, lieutenant-colonel. – Philipe Reyly, major. – Bryan Reyly, ayde-major.- Hugh Reyly, aumosnier. – Luke Tully, chirurgien. – Ed: Smith, quartier-maître.

Régiment de Slane

Capitaines	*Lieutenants*	*Enseignes*	*Hommes effectifs*
Brouder, grenadier	Hill et Wigmore	–	42
My lord Slane, colonel	Nagle	Flemin	30
Le sieur Connell, lieut.-colonel	Burne	Connell	38
Veldon	Bathe	Walters	34
Everard	Misset	Flaide	46
Cruise	Gorman	Flemin	44
Joanes	Toule	Holahan	34
De L 'Osier	Talbot	–	27
Conly	Bedlew	Delahoide	35
Barry	Flemin	Barry	34
Barnewal	Burford	Nolan	31

Capitaines	*Lieutenants*	*Enseignes*	*Hommes effectifs*
Luke Everard	Cusack	Urel	40
Cusack	Bath	Usher	45
Chivers	Le sieur Stokes	Brett	32
Kelly	Trant	Kenric	39
Plus: quarante-deux hommes de recrue arrivés après la revue			42
15	16	13	593

Estat major : – My lord Slane, colonel. – Le sieur Connell, lieutenant-colonel. – Le sieur Fressieu, lieutenant-colonel en second. – Le sieur Fitz Gerald, major. – Le sieur Gorman, ayde-major. – Le sieur Flemin, maréchal des logis. – Le sieur Montet, chirurgien. – Le sieur Everard, aumosnier.

Officers à la suitte de dit régiment : – Capitaines : Le sieur Gould, le sieur Milleau, le sieur Duplanbrideron, le sieur Bernard, le sieur Belliquier de Jarnacq. Lieutenants : Le sieur De Tel, le sieur Goghagan, le sieur Rue.

Régiment de Tirone

Capitaines	*Lieutenants*	*Enseignes*	*Hommes effectifs*
MacNamara, grenadier	Ronain, Morphy	–	63
Le Comte de Tyrone	Girardin	Power	69
Nugent, lieut.-colonel	Power	Russell	70
Kerts	Power	–	57
Power	Wilson	Power	72
Burne	Rice	Valois	71
Walsh	Morphy	–	69
Comerford	Briens	Aylmer	71
Val. Walsh	Nugent	Walsh	65
Cruise	Preston	Nugent	64
Macartie	Roussel	–	70
Magrah	Brien	Dennis Bryen	70
Fitz Gerald	Nagle	Welsh	63
13	14	9	874

Estat major: – Le comte de Tyrone, colonel. – Le sieur Nugent, lieutenant-colonel. – Le sieur Nagle, major. – Le sieur Power, ayde-major. – Le sieur Swyny, maréchal des logis. – Le sieur Guilleau Walsh, ausmonier. – Le sieur Comerford, chirurgien. – Magrah, tambour-major.

Régiment de Westmeath

Capitaines	*Lieutenants*	*Enseignes*	*Hommes effectifs*
My lord Westmeath, colonel	–	-	50
Wuckain	–	-	58
Walsh	–	-	62
Brinain	–	-	49
Charles Toole	–	-	49
Jean Birne	–	-	57
Garret Birne	–	-	66
Cowdell	–	-	68
Meade	–	-	73
Doyle	–	-	57
Nevill	–	-	51
Whitburne	–	-	75
Blackburne	–	-	59
Toole	–	-	814
14			

Estat major: – My lord Westmeath, colonel. – François Toole, lieutenant-colonel. – De la Hoyde, major. – Dennis Birne, ayde-major. – Higuier Preston, maréchal des logis et lieutenant réformé. – Brian, aumosnier. – Tully, chirurgien. – De la Barre, capitaine à la suitte. – Le sieur Merryman, enseigne.

ESTAT DE LA CAVALLERIE DU ROY

Régiment d' Abricorne [Abricorne]

Capitaines	*Lieutenants*	*Cornettes*	*Maréchaux des logis*	*Cavalliers*
My lord Abricorne, colonel	Clinch	Luby	Dwyer	45
Rice	O'Bryen	Heffernan	Buttler	48
Aylmor	Bedlew	Hamlim	Neale	41
Goghagan	De Lisle	Goghagan	Johnings	43
Dillon	Burk	–	–	37
5	5	4	4	214

Estat major : – My lord Abricorne, colonel. – Corbert, major. – Cooke, ayde-major. – Dowdal, aumosnier. – Fitz Patrick, chirurgien.

Officers à la suitte du dit régiment : – Bingam, Prendergast. – Lieutenants : Brackston, L'espine. – Cornette : Roberts.

Régiment de dragons de Cotter

Capitaines	*Lieutenants*	*Cornettes*	*Maréchaux des logis*	*Dragons*
M. Cotter, colonel	Fitz Gerald	O'Brien	Barry	52
Le sieur Lacy	Moore	Hagan	–	25
Le sieur Power	Burk	Kenedy	–	38
Le sieur Barry	Moore	Lacy	–	39
Le sieur Coppinger	Coppinger	Barry	–	36
Le sieur Gallwey	Barry	Collins	Coppinger	30
Le sieur Wanelle	Lycet	Goulde	–	27
Le sieur Taylor	Keruan	Linch	Batkin	30
Le sieur Grand	Barry	Wilson	Baker	38
Le sieur Trant, lieut.-colonel	Gallouay	Periman	Meskell	38
10	10	10	5	353

Estat major : – M. Cotter, colonel. – M. Trant, lieutenant-colonel. – Le sieur Carol, major. – Le sieur O'Brien, ayde-major. – Le sieur Barry, maréchal des logis. – Le sieur Barry, aumosnier. – Le sieur Tryaden, chirurgien.

Régiment de dragons de Clifford

Capitaines	*Lieutenants*	*Cornettes*	*Maréchaux des logis*	*Dragons*
Le sieur Clifford, colonel	Fox	Burk	–	28
Buttler	Carny	Boyton	Mulhaly	29
Ware	Tyrel	Clifford	Doyle	30
Dalton	Dalton	Smith	–	27
Foster	Keruan	Mathews	Flangan	25
Makensy	Burton	Fitz Gerald	Fitz Gerald	26
Makensy, lieut.-colonel	Connor	Dufresne	–	27
Gibbons	Gallaghan	Gibbons	–	27
Faril	Burne	Faril	Griffin	57
Coghlan	Ferret	Daly	Goghagan	49
10	10	10	6	325

Estat major : M. Clifford, colonel. – Baron de Morle, lieutenant-colonel. – Burk, major. – Lanaghan, ayde-major et quartier-maître. – Tully, chirurgien. – Doyle, aumosnier.

Officers à la suitte du régiment : – Capitaines : Crofton, Stich. – Lieutenants : Richardson, King, Chamberlain, Clifford. – Quartier-maîtres : Burk, le sieur Oar.

Régiment de dragons de Dungan

Capitaines	*Lieutenants*	*Cornettes*	*Maréchaux des logis*	*Dragons*
My lord Dungan, colonel	Cavenagh	Iky	Morphy	55
Pierrespol	Archbold	Dungan	Stragan	47
Neugent	Mepas	Archbold	Comerford	50
Cokely	Eustace	Cokely	Morphy	63
G. Archbold	Archbold	Fitz Gerald	Boors	65
Horly	Darsy	Price	Delmero	49
Bellew	Talbot	Bellew	Boorun	53
Plunket	Talbot	Fitz Gerald	Netorfield	56
Royard Bellew	P. Bellew	P. Bellew	Tho. Bodel	48
Carol, lieutenant colonel	Jean Halland	Higins	Carol	53
10	10	10	539	

Officers réformés : – De Corday, capitaine ; Delle, Demsy, lieutenants : Buttler, Corn. Obrun, cornettes : Kelly, maréchal des logis.

Estat major : – My lord Dungan, colonel. – M. Caroll, lieutenant-colonel.

Régiment de cavallerie de Galmoy

Capitaines	*Lieutenants*	*Cornettes*	*Maréchaux des logis*	*Cavallerie*
My lord Galmoy	Gerlons	Carol	Nachy	41
Oxburg	Purcell	Dwyer	Pordon	36
Butler	Girardin	Connor	Fitz Gerald	42
Arthur	Fitz Gerald	Walsh	Russel	41
Flemin	Alyn	Burk	Butler	38
Caroly	Mathews	Rene	Burk	44
Tramleston	Carney	Mouloy	Buttler	50
Demsy, lieut.-colonel	Cooke	Dulhanty	Connor	46
8	8	8	8	338

Estat major : – My lord Galmoy, colonel. – M. Dempsy, lieutenant-colonel. – M. De Boissevert, François, lieutenant-colonel. – M. Major Carol. – Allin, ayde-major. – Rene, maréchal des logis. – St. Jean, chirurgien. – Cusacq, aumosnier.

Officers à la suitte du régiment : – De Cullon, Danferuet, Devillemense, capitaines François: Cony, capitaine Irlandois: Couenant, Delavallete, Soulegre, Caroly, De Louche, lieutenants François: Hagan, Magin, maréchaux des logis.

Régiment de cavallerie de Luttrell

Capitaines	*Lieutenants*	*Cornettes*	*Maréchaux des logis*	*Cavallerie*
Le sieur Luttrell, colonel	Barnewal	Collins	St. Johns	91
Le sieur Maurice	Maurice	Power	Flemin	38
Le sieur Connor	Kelly	Farmer	Mouloy	35
Le sieur Lawlesse	Le sieur Burk	Dowan	Fanin	33
Le sieur Dorsy	Wall	Chapman	Carew	31
5	5	5	5	228

Estat major : – Monsieur Luttrell, colonel. – Le chevallier Moclar, lieutenant-colonel. – Le sieur Misleaux, lieutenant-colonel en second. – Le sieur Sainte Croix, major. – Le sieur Barry, ayde-major. – Le sieur Macdaniel, aumosnier. – Le sieur White, chirurgien.

Officers à la suitte du régiment : – Le comte de Tressesson, capitaine François. – Le sieur Nugent, capitaine. – Le sieur Kenedy, le sieur Carpentier, lieutenants.

Régiment de dragons de Luttrell

Capitaines	*Lieutenants*	*Cornettes*	–	*Dragons*
Blaye	French	Daly	–	51
Grace	Harches	Brady	–	50
P. Bellew	Doudal	V [acante]	–	50
Tyrel	Meyt	De Kemfil	–	59
Flemin	Bestard	Warrin	–	53
Broalls	Connel	Carter	St Jean	56
Londres	Barnewal	Magdaniel	Suetman	55
7	7	6	2	374

Estat major : -- M. Luttrel, colonel. – Goghagan, lieutenant-colonel. – Desançons, autre lieutenant-colonel. – Moclar, major. – Quin, ayde-major. – Chirequn, maréchal des logis. – Le chirurgien. – L'aumosnier. – Le sieur Maguire, lieutenant en second.

Les Gardes du Corps
[Blank]
Régiment de dragons de Maxvil [Maxwell]

Capitaines	*Lieutenants*	*Cornettes*	*Maréchaux des logis*	*Dragons*
Le sieur Maxuell, colonel	Sauvage	Sauvage	Magon	55
Maginis	Maginis	Garney	–	47
Trogmorton	Dermot	Trogmorton	Tungard	55
Mackarten	Mackarten	Mackarten	Burne	55
Savage	Savage	Savage	Savage	53
O'Neale	Calanan	Magenis	–	53
My lord Howard	Clancy	Brien, Maclaly	–	56
Alaury	Alaury	Alaury	Magny	56
Dunkin	Roger	Macarton	Magdaniel	56
Cook	Lahonty	Cook	Mizi	49
Macmoelin	Macmollin	Dohorty	Savage	56
Cusack	Mageny	Daubin	Daubin	56
12	12	12	8	649

Estat major : – M. Maxuelle, colonel. – Daniel Magenis, lieutenant-colonel. – D. Calahan, major. – Charles, ayde-major. – chirurgien. – aumosnier.

Régiment de dragons de N. O'Neale

Capitaines	*Lieutenants*	*Cornettes*	*Maréchaux des logis*	*Dragons*
Le chevallier O'Neale	Terence O'Neale	Maurice	Hiky	29
Maginis	Makane	–	Manerin	45
Tarnan	Lemineur	Dillon	J. Sales	22
Savage	Savage	Savage	Burne	39
O'Neale, senior	Goghagan	Felim O'Neale	Connell	37
Henry O'Neale	Law	Sales	Burne	30
Maginis	Macartie	–	Tole Carney	35
Buttler	Ready	Buttler	Kelly	37
Eustace	Eustace	Grahams	Egan	42
Geoffry Favé	Pierse	Darcei	Gerardin	27
Girardin	Guilleaume	Buttler	Grace	49
11	11	9	11	392

Estat major : – Le chevallier O'Neale, colonel. – Le sieur Tallendier, lieutenant-colonel. – Ryordin, major. – Le sieur Tarneau, major en second. – Le sieur Hederman, ayde-major. – Le sieur Hughs, aumosnier. – Le sieur Jean Telliar, chirurgien.

Régiment de dragons d' O'Brien

Capitaines	*Lieutenants*	*Cornettes*	*Maréchaux des logis*	*Dragons*
O'Brien, colonel	O'Brien	Fitzgerald	Kilean	–
Kilaha	Pursell	Malking	Macnamara	–
O'Brien	Ifcher	Hogan	Adea	–
Mahon	Kerly	Perry	Hehir	–
Gerard	Nayler	Lusagh	Macnamara	–
Macnamara	Hurly	Nogane	Wise	–
O'Brien	Bedford	Clancy	Leo	–
Purdon	Bedingfield	Burk	Fitzgerald	–
Daniel	Cahane	Archdeacon	Bohelly	–
Slaugh	Furlong	Dean	Sulevant	–
Philippes, lieut.-colonel	Barry	Fitzgerald	Hanford	–
11	11	11	11	

Estat major : – O'Bryen, colonel. – Philippes, lieutenant-colonel. – Frayne, major. – Deron, ayde-major. – Daly, aumosnier. – Barry, quartier-maître. – Nelan, chirurgien.

Régiment de cavallerie de Parker

Capitaines	*Lieutenants*	*Cornettes*	*Maréchaux des logis*	*Br.et Cavalliers*
Parker, colonel	Greene	Hells	Cornefort	56
D'Adington	Binfield	St. Clair	Cacklend	54
De Clistois	Charnu	Vacante	Baufin	51
Dudrington	Marechal	Maston	Seluy	54
D'Estens	Talbot	Tessony	Soliman	54
Hebb	Fermor	Beaupré	Estrich	54
Neugent	Lagardie	La Tardiere	Ill	54
Devimency	Lock	Semalbons	Haekler	54
8	8	7	7	431

Officers réformés : – Power, D'touilly, capitaines : Girardiere, lieutenant.

Estat major : – M. Parker, colonel. – Devimency, lieutenant-colonel. – Natton. major. – Dielle, ayde-major. – Kelly, maréchal des logis. – Hoette, Traps, chaplaines. – Hardin, chirurgien.

Régiment de dragons de Pursell

Capitaines	*Lieutenants*	*Cornettes*	*Maréchaux des logis*	*Dragons*
Purcell, colonel	Butler	Bavan	–	40
Purcell, lieutenant-colonel	Purcell	Purcell	–	45
Everard	Traverse	Fitz patrick	–	31
Pursell	Pursell	Pursell	–	21
Buttler	Coning	Nihil	–	31
Macartie	Power	Macarty	–	36
Fitz Gerald	Maker	Maker	–	26
Condon	Geraldin	Maly	–	36
Cantwell	Condon	Hurly	–	40
Morice	Kenedy	Kenedy	–	25
Ed. Morice	Ryan	Keatin	–	44
Tobin	Buttler	Merick	–	44
12	12	12	–	419

Estat major : – M. Pursell, colonel. – Purcell, lieutenant-colonel. – MacDaniel, major. – Ryan, ayde-major. – Buttler, maréchal des logis. – Dylany, aumosnier. – Le chirurgien,

Régiment de Sarsfield: cavallerie

Capitaines	*Lieutenants*	*Cornettes*	*Cavalliers*
M. Sarsfield, colonel	Nugent	Plunket	54
Le sieur Nagle, capitaine	Tyrel	Wren	33
Le sieur O'Neale	La Mezadiere	Pursell	40
Carny	Lester	Fitz Gerald	42
Burk, Jean	St. Archange	Maurice	53
Guydon	Sarsfield	Doudal	46
Tho. Burk	Burk	Dillon	41
Macnamara	Buttler	Burk	50
My lord Kinsale	St John	Taafe	37
9	9	9	396

Estat major : – Monsieur Sarsfield, colonel. – My lord Kingsale, lieutenant-colonel. – Magueligan, major. – St. Archange, ayde-major. – Lane, quartier-maître. – Magrah, capitaine en second. – Burke, capitaine. – Tute, lieutenant. – Macarty, maréchal des logis réformé. --, chaplaine. --, chirurgien. – Brag, maréchal des logis en second.

Régiment de cavallerie de Sutherland

Capitaines	*Lieutenants*	*Cornettes*	*Maréchaux des logis*	*Cavalliers*
Wray	Daniel	Prendergast	Ryan	42
Mathews	Mathews	Ryan	Mathews	46
Bryan	Rothe	–	-	42
Callaghan	Coningham	Verdon	Coningham	54
4	4	3	3	184

Estat major : – Monsieur Sutherland, colonel. – Prendergast, lieutenant-colonel. – Oglethorpe, ayde-major.

Régiment de cavallerie de Tyrconell

Capitaines	*Lieutenants*	*Cornettes*	*Maréchaux des logis*
My lord Tyrconnel, colonel	Byetagh	Nugent	Colene
Arthur	Burk	Avny	Walsh
Belleu	Jacqueman	Furlon	Cavenagh
Cusacq	Barnewal	Taafe	Cusacq
Meara	King	Nugent	Mutus
Howard	Roche	Roche	Strongman
Chevallier Tuck	Kirk	Buttler	Faril
Crosby	Denis	Creagh	St. Leger
Sheldon, lieutenant-colonel	Kealing	Buttler	Bryan
9	9	9	9

Estat major : – My lord Tyrconnell, colonel. – M. Sheldon, lieutenant-colonel. – M. Nugent, major. – Buttler, ayde-major. – Mackalaster, quartier-maître. – Power, chirurgien. – Le sieur Taafe, aumosnier.

Officers à la suitte : – Stafely, Devalancy, De Bada, De Sompuy, Keralie, Creagh, capitaines : De Bourdenance, lieutenant.

Notes on Sources

KEYS TO LETTERS IN THE TEXT

[A] *Journal of John Stevens*
John Stevens was an English Catholic who followed James to France and took part in the war as a Captain in the Grand Prior's regiment. He never fired a shot at the Boyne, was hit on the head by a stone at Athlone, took part in the defence of the inner barricade at the first siege of Limerick and, alas, his journal does not cover Aughrim. He was present and survived to write his journal. The edition I have used is the 1912 edition published in Oxford.

[B] Murray, R.H.Revd. *Revolutionary Ireland and Its Settlement* (London 1911)
This account is based on contemporary sources like O'Kelly, Berwick, Clarke and D'Avaux and has some excellent maps.

[C] Burnet, G. (Bishop of Salisbury) *History Of My Own Time* (6 Vols, Oxford,1823)
Burnet is not a good military historian but he gives a good overall impression of events and he knows most of the important people at the time.

[D] P.R.O. The Public Records Office has the Committee on Ireland minutes (WO/55/339) and the correspondence from Ireland (WO/55/1794). The two together provide an interesting picture of the way military events and supplies etc. were organised.

[E] *Calendar of State Papers* Edited by W. Hardy, (5 Vols. London 1689 – 95)

[F] Plunket *A Light to the Blind*
This is a fascinating account by an unknown Jacobite on the wars. I have used the reprint edition with an introduction by J.G.Simms.

[G] Wauchope, P. *Patrick Sarsfield and the Williamite War* Dublin, 1992
A very scholarly account of Sarsfield's contribution to events with useful notes and bibliography.

[H] Boulger, D.C. *The Battle of the Boyne* London, 1911
A useful book with many French sources, very anti-Macaulay.

[J] Sergeant, P.W. *Little Jennings and Fighting Dick Talbot* (2 Vols. London 1913)
Has Tyrconnell's letters, Stevens' account of the Boyne, and makes some shrewd, if over-long judgements.

[K] Colomb, P.H., Vice-Admiral *Naval Warfare* London, 1899
Includes Torrington's defence.

[L] *Irish Sword* – See Bibliography for details.

Bibliography

Bartlett, T. and Jeffery, K. (Editors), *A Military History of Ireland,* Cambridge, 1996.
Boyce, D.G. and O'Day, *The Making of Modern Irish History,* London, 1996.
Buchan, J, *The Nations of Today: Ireland,* London, 1929. (Editors: Murray, R.H. and Law, H.)
Burnet, Bishop, *History of His Own Time* (6 Vols). Oxford, 1823.
Childs, J. *The British Army of William III.* Manchester, 1977.
Clark, G.N. *The Later Stuarts.* (2nd Edition) Oxford, 1955.
Churchill, W. *Marlborough, His Life and Times.* (2 Vols.) London, 1947.
Clifford, B. *Derry and the Boyne* (Plunket). Belfast, 1990. (Includes selections from *A Light to the Blind.)*
Colomb, P.H., Vice-Admiral, *Naval Warfare.* London, 1899.
De Beer, E.S. (Editor) *The Diary of John Evelyn.* Oxford, 1959.
Ditzhuyzen, Reina Van *Het Huis Van Oranje.* Haarlem, 1979.
Ehrman, J. *The Navy in the War of William III.* Cambridge, 1953.
Ellis, P.B. *The Boyne Water.* London, 1976.
Foster, R.F.(Editor) *The Oxford Illustrated History of Ireland.* Oxford, 1989.
Foster, R.F.*Modern Ireland 1600–1972.* London, 1988.
Hayes-McCoy, G.A. *Irish Battles.* Belfast, 1989.
Hoak, D, and Feingold, M. *Anglo-Dutch Perspectives on the Revolution of 1688–9.* Stanford, 1996.
Horwitz, H. (Editor) *Parliamentary Diary of Narcissus Luttrell 1691–3.* Oxford, 1972.
Horwitz, H. *Parliament, Policy and Politics in the Reign of William III.* Manchester, 1977.
Kishlansky, M. *A Monarchy Transformed – Britain 1603–1714.* London,1996.
Macaulay, T.B. *The History of England from the Accession of James II in 3 Volumes.* London, 1966 Edition.
Miller, J. *The Life and Times of William and Mary.* London, 1974
Murray, J.H. *Revolutionary Ireland and its Settlements.* London, 1911.
Murray, R.H. *The Journal of John Stevens.* Oxford, 1912.
Ogg, David. *England in the Reigns of James II and William III.* Oxford, 1955.
Petrie, Charles Sir. *The Jacobite Movement.* London, 1959.
Shepherd, R. *Ireland's Fate.* London, 1990.
Simms, J.G. *Jacobite Ireland.* London, 1969.
Simms, J.G. *The Williamite Confiscation in Ireland, 1690–1703.* London, 1956.
Trevor, M. *The Shadow of a Crown – Life Story of James II.* London, 1988.
Wauchope, P. *Patrick Sarsfield and the Williamite War.* Blackrock, 1992.

LEAFLETS

There are several useful leaflets, such as *The Boyne* (O'Boyle), *Aughrim* (Guidebook) which are worth consulting as well as the excellent diorama at the Aughrim Battlefield Centre.

ORIGINAL SOURCES

Calendar of State Papers Domestic 1688–1692
WO/55/339 Committee for Ireland Minutes
WO/55/1794 Correspondence from Ireland

JOURNALS

THE IRISH SWORD

1949/50	Vol.I, No.1.	Magan-Sarsfield's defence of the Shannon. 1690–91.
1950/51	Vol.I, No.2.	Garland – The Regiment of MacElligott 1688–9. Replies 157. Scott/MacElligott
1958	Vol.III, No.12	Tohall. Charlemont Fort, Co.Armagh.
1960	Vol.IV, No.16	O'Danachair. Report of a (Danish) Cavalry Action, April, 1691.
1961	Vol.V, No.18.	O'Danachair. The Danish Corps in Ireland 1690–91.
1971	Vol.X, No.39.	Melvin. Irish Troop movements and James II's army in 1688.
1990	Vol.XVIII, No.70.	Murtagh, D & H. Irish Jacobite Army 1698–91 O'Carroll. Battlefield of the Boyne. Harrington. Images of the Boyne. Ferguson. Organisation of King William's Army in Ireland, 1689–92.

HISTORY TODAY

1988, August. Childs, J. A Patriot for Whom? For God and For Honour – Marshal Schomberg.

Index

MILITARY HISTORY BOOKS

THE LETTERS OF PRIVATE WHEELER 1809–1828
An eyewitness account of the Battle of Waterloo
Edited and with a foreword by B. H. Liddell Hart
'Vivid images – of people, landscape, events – flow from his pen . . . one of military history's great originals'
John Keegan
Paperback £9.99

THE DIARY OF A NAPOLEONIC FOOT SOLDIER
Jakob Walter
A conscript in the *Grande Armée's* account of the long march home on the retreat from Moscow
Edited and Introduced by Mark Raeff
Paperback £9.99 Illustrated

THE RECOLLECTIONS OF RIFLEMAN HARRIS
One of the most popular military books of all time.
Edited and Introduced by Christopher Hibbert
'Describing narrow squeaks and terrible deprivations, Harris's account of fortitude and resilience in Spain still bristles with a freshness and an invigorating spikiness.'
Scotland on Sunday
'An ordinary soldier's memoirs are rare but precious. Harris's are a most vivid record of the war in Spain and Portugal against Napoleon, the same campaign as featured in the recent TV drama series, 'Sharpe'.'
The Mail on Sunday
Paperback £9.99

A SOLDIER OF THE SEVENTY-FIRST
The journal of a Soldier in the Peninsular War
Edited and Introduced by Christopher Hibbert
'His elegant style and his descriptive power take us with him at every step.'
The Sunday Telegraph
Paperback £9.99

THE WHEATLEY DIARY
A Journal & Sketchbook from the Peninsular War & The Waterloo Campaign
Edited and Introduced by Christopher Hibbert
Paperback £10.99 Illustrated in colour

THE RECOLLECTIONS OF SERGEANT MORRIS
A Cockney Soldier at Waterloo
Edited by John Selby
Paperback £9.99